WELCOME 3

Hans G. Hoffmann
Patricia Mugglestone

WELCOME 3

Englischkurs für Erwachsene

Lehrbuch

Max Hueber Verlag

Hans G. Hoffmann · Patricia Mugglestone
Welcome 3
Englischkurs für Erwachsene
Lehrbuch

Materialbeschaffung und Recherchen:
Brigitte Hoffmann
Sprachliche Durchsicht und Beratung:
Hilary Heltay, Brian Aiken
Phonetische Durchsicht und Beratung:
Graham Pascoe
Verlagsredaktion: John Stevens
Umschlag: Atelier Stark und Klingshirn, München
Typographie und Layout: Rudolf P. Gorbach
Projektleitung: Heinrich Schrand

Redaktionsschluß der 1. Auflage: März 1983

Dieses Lehrwerk berücksichtigt die vom Deutschen Volkshochschul-Verband entwickelten Lernzielkataloge zum Grundbaustein und VHS-Zertifikat Englisch.

1. Auflage

5. 4. 3.
1991 90 89 88 87
Die letzten Ziffern bezeichnen Zahl und Jahr des Druckes.
Alle Drucke dieser Auflage können, da unverändert, nebeneinander benutzt werden.

Gesamtherstellung: Druckerei Auer, Donauwörth
Printed in Germany
ISBN 3-19-002293-3

CIP-Kurztitelaufnahme der Deutschen Bibliothek

Welcome : Englischkurs für Erwachsene / Hans G. Hoffmann; Patricia Mugglestone. – München [i.e. Ismaning] : Hueber

NE: Hoffmann, Hans G. [Mitverf.]

3.
Lehrbuch. – 1. Aufl. – 1983.

ISBN 3–19–002293–3

Vorwort

Welcome ist ein dreibändiges Lehrwerk, das Anfänger bei flacher Progression schnell zu praktisch verwertbaren Englischkenntnissen führt.
Der erste Band vermittelt einen Grundwortschatz von 800 Wörtern und die wichtigsten Wortformen und Satzstrukturen. Nach Erarbeitung dieses Stoffes kann der Lernende bereits Gespräche über einfache Alltagsthemen führen und einfache Privatbriefe schreiben.
Der zweite Band erweitert den Wortschatz um knapp 1000 Wörter und fördert den Lernenden in allen Bereichen der Sprachanwendung bis zum Niveau des vom Deutschen Volkshochschul-Verband definierten Grundbausteins[1]. Die Erreichung dieses Lernziels kann durch Ablegung einer Prüfung unter Beweis gestellt werden.
Der vorliegende dritte Band führt mit 940 zusätzlichen Wörtern zum Kenntnis- und Fertigkeitsstand des Volkshochschul-Zertifikats Englisch 1[2], das ungefähr dem mittleren Schulabschluß für Englisch entspricht und nach dessen Erreichung ebenfalls ein Prüfungszeugnis erworben werden kann.
Jede der 15 Units des vorliegenden Buches bietet Stoff für ca. 180 Minuten Kursunterricht. Das begleitende Arbeitsbuch enthält mannigfaltige zusätzliche Übungen, die wegen des beigegebenen Lösungsschlüssels vom Lernenden allein, ohne Hilfe des Lehrers, durchgenommen werden können, sich aber auch für eine Anreicherung des Gruppenunterrichts eignen.
Die Units dieses Lehrbuches sind durchweg einsprachig englisch gehalten. Die textliche und graphische Gestaltung ermöglicht einen lebendigen, erwachsenengemäßen Unterricht, in welchem Hör-, Sprech-, Lese- und Schreibaktivitäten einander in rascher Folge abwechseln.
Für die individuelle Nacharbeit bieten sich im Anhang des Lehrbuches zahlreiche Verzeichnisse, Listen und Übersichten an, die ganz auf die Lern- und Nachschlagebedürfnisse von Deutschsprachigen abgestimmt sind. Zu den im Lehrbuch und im Arbeitsbuch mit [Cassette] gekennzeichneten Texten und Übungen liegen Tonaufnahmen auf Cassetten und Tonbändern vor, die teils für den Gruppenunterricht und teils für das individuelle Lernen gedacht sind. Auch die zu *Welcome* entwickelten Lernwörterbücher und die den Lehrbüchern beigegebenen Grammatikkarten sind geeignet, den Lernprozeß zu intensivieren, zu rationalisieren und zu beschleunigen.
Für die didaktische Gestaltung dieses Lehrwerks haben die Grundlagenarbeiten der Pädagogischen Arbeitsstelle des Deutschen Volkshochschul-Verbandes wichtige Voraussetzungen geschaffen. Wesentliche Impulse gingen von der Fachdiskussion aus, wie sie auf Lehrertagungen in Deutschland, Österreich und der Schweiz und in Zeitschriften geführt wurde.

Verfasser und Verlag

[1] *Grundbaustein zum VHS-Zertifikat Englisch,* Deutscher Volkshochschul-Verband 1980
[2] *Das VHS-Zertifikat Englisch,* Deutscher Volkshochschul-Verband 1977

Abkürzungen und Symbole

In diesem Buch werden folgende Abkürzungen und Symbole benutzt:

AE	bedeutet: Amerikanisches Englisch (*American English*)
BE	bedeutet: Britisches Englisch (*British English*)
Austral.	bedeutet: Australisches Englisch (*Australian English*)
[Kassettensymbol]	bedeutet: Zu dem betreffenden Abschnitt liegen Tonaufnahmen vor
[Schreibsymbol]	bedeutet: Der Abschnitt ist für handschriftliche Eintragungen des/der Lernenden eingerichtet, die jedoch unterbleiben müssen, wenn es sich bei dem vorliegenden Buch um ein im Rahmen der Lernmittelfreiheit leihweise überlassenes Exemplar handelt
(→ G4)	bedeutet: Siehe Abschnitt G4 in der *Englischen Grammatik im Überblick* im Anhang
(→ 15D2)	bedeutet: Siehe Abschnitt D2 in Unit 15

Quellenverzeichnis

Der Verlag dankt den folgenden Personen, Institutionen und Unternehmen für ihre freundliche Genehmigung zum Abdruck von Copyright-Material:

Campaign for Nuclear Disarmament (Bristol): Fotos S. 40, 41
Daily Telegraph / Bill Wood (London): Foto S. 21
Fricke Public-Relations-Beratung (Mettmann): Foto S. 59
Haus Haard (Oer-Erkenschwick): Foto S. 42
Hoffmann (Windeck): Fotos S. 10, 11, 16, 17, 19, 24, 26, 27, 29, 32, 33, 34, 35, 43, 44, 45, 46, 47, 48, 49, 57, 58, 60, 62, 70, 71, 74, 75 (unten)
Felicitas Hübner (München): Zeichnungen S. 22–23, 36–37, 50–51, 64–65
Dr. Konrad Karkosch (München): Foto S. 55
Keystone Pressedienst (Hamburg): Foto S. 52
Monitor Picture Library (London): Foto S. 28
George Philip & Son Ltd (London): Landkarte S. 78–79
Punch / Werner Lüning (Lübeck): Cartoons S. 13, 14, 20, 25, 30, 31, 44, 53, 61, 69, 73, 77
Royal Society for the Prevention of Cruelty to Animals (London): Foto S. 63
San Jose Mercury News (San Jose): Zeichnung S. 39
Marion Schweitzer / Rex Features (München): Foto S. 75 (oben)
Veronica Sharp, The Order of St. John (London): Foto S. 69
Süddeutscher Verlag (München): Foto S. 38
Syndication International Ltd (London): Foto S. 18

Inhaltsverzeichnis

Unit	Redeabsichten	Themen Situationen	Grammatik	Seite
1 Classroom opinion poll An after-dinner chat World weather	Berichtend reden; jem. befragen; Gewohnheiten/ Wünsche ausdrücken; Aussagen salopp verstärken; Sachverhalte werbend formulieren; Bedingung ausdrücken; argumentativ reden	Urlaub/Ferien Wetter Briefliche Hotelbuchung	Bedingungssätze Typ 1 und 2	10
2 Drunk driver learns lesson At the pub Talking about news items 12-year-old worried by drinking parents	Zeugenaussage machen; Anklage formulieren; sich verteidigen; berichtend reden; Problem darstellen u. Rat erbitten; Vorschläge machen; jem. gut zureden	Trunkenheit am Steuer Vor Gericht In der Gaststätte Alkohol u. seine Probleme	Perfekt f. noch andauernde Handlungen Bedingungssätze Typ 2	14
3 On the ball from nine to five Working while others sleep Making her own way Willing to do anything	Aussage bestätigen; Gewohnheit, Bereitschaft ausdrücken; beschreiben; Sachverhalt kommentieren; Vergleiche anstellen	Arbeitswelt Arbeitslosigkeit Stellenmarkt Briefl. Bewerbung	*so/nor do/can/ am/ . . . I* *-ing* nach Präposition	18
Time for a break 1				22
4 What would you have done? Making a complaint On the art of complaining	Eigene Handlungen in hypothetischen Situationen ausdrücken; sich mündl. od. schriftl. beschweren; etw. reklamieren	Im Geschäft: Kunde/Kundin – Verkäufer(in) Beschwerde, Reklamation mündl. u. schriftl.	Bedingungssätze Typ 3 Infin. d. Perf. *should(n't) have* + Part. Perf. Relativsätze	24
5 The Hatton Garden bank raid	Berichtend reden; Rückfragen stellen; Vermutungen ausdrücken; Mitteilungen kommentieren; Informationen erfragen; Sachbericht formulieren	Bankraub Interview	Modalverb + *have* + Partizip Perf. Bedingungssätze Typ 3	28

6 Choices and decisions A letter from Australia	Präferenzen ausdrücken u. begründen; Verhalten in hypothetischen Situationen verbalisieren	Australien als Tourismusziel Briefwechsel nach einer Urlaubsreise Die eigene Umwelt als Tourismusziel	Relativsätze u. attributiv gebrauchte Infinitiv- u. *-ing*-Strukturen	32
Time for a break 2				36
7 A modern dilemma	Zu einem Problem kontroverse Standpunkte vertreten; Meinungsverschiedenheit u. -übereinstimmung ausdrücken	Nukleare Bedrohung Rüstungswettlauf Friedenssicherung	Partizip Perf. als Attribut Kongruenz im Numerus Perfekt	38
8 Finding the right class Never too old to learn A circular letter	Informationen erfragen; Wünsche verbalisieren; Mutmaßung, eigene Meinung äußern; zu überzeugen versuchen	Erwachsenenbildung Sprachunterricht Werbebrief Briefl. Anfrage	*-ly*-Adverbien Infinitiv *-ing*-Form	42
9 Getting things done Old folk victims of teenage terror The new playground	Notwendigkeit, Absicht, Wunsch, Neigung ausdrücken; Furcht, Beeinträchtigung, Protest ausdrücken; pro u. contra argumentieren; Probleme artikulieren	Dienstleistungen Generationsprobleme Beschädigung Öffentl. Ordnung Diskussion v. Sozialeinrichtungen	*have/get something done* Verb + Obj. + Inf./*-ing*	46
Time for a break 3				50
10 Predicting what lies ahead Glimpses of the future? Orwell's 1984	Zukunftsaussagen machen; Meinung, Unsicherheit, Möglichkeit artikulieren; Meinungsäußerungen kommentieren	Zukunftsprognosen Orwells Anti-Utopia	Futur Indirekte Rede Bedingungssätze Typ 3 u. 2	52
11 Grand puzzle A letter from David	Persönl. Erlebnis berichten; techn. Gegenstand beschreiben; auf eine Äußerung reagieren; pro u. contra argumentieren	Privatbrief Unfallbericht Elektron. Kleingeräte Verkaufsgespräch	*some – any* Relativsätze	56

12 Changing eating habits Vegetarianism – pros and cons	Kontrovers argumentieren; Stellung nehmen, Meinung äußern	Ernährungsformen Trends Vegetarismus	Bedingungssätze Typ 3 u. 2 *-ly*-Adverbien *so/nor do/am/... I*	60
Time for a break 4				64
13 Handguns banned in San Francisco Georgia city outlaws non-possession of guns	Vergleiche ausdrücken; Fakten rekapitulieren u. kommentieren; Entrüstung, Widerspruch, Verwunderung ausdrücken; argumentativ diskutieren	Das Recht auf Schußwaffenbesitz	*-self*-Pronomen: Gebrauch u. Nichtgebrauch	66
14 Talking about yourself Back from a vacation Letter from Illinois	Auf persönl. Mitteilungen reagieren; Dank, Freude, Sympathie ausdrücken; Einladung formulieren; persönl. Probleme artikulieren; Mutmaßungen ausdrücken	Beantwortung informeller Briefe Familienneuigkeiten Amerik. Englisch	Gebrauch d. Tempora	70
15 Dismissed for swearing at the boss Failing to obey the lights The dog that came back from the dead	In einem Konflikt Partei nehmen; Aussagen üb. eigenes Verhalten in hypothet. Situationen machen; Mutmaßungen ausdrükken; sich m. jem. auseinandersetzen; Kritik ausdrücken; sich/andere rechtfertigen	Öffentl. Schilder interpretieren Alltagskonflikte	Bedingungssätze Typ 3 Frageanhängsel Kurzantworten	74

Anhang

Landkarte: The world 78
Wörterverzeichnis nach Units 80
Wendungen für das Alltagsgespräch (Redeabsichten/Sprechintentionen) . 104
Englische Grammatik im Überblick . 106
Namenverzeichnis 113
Grammatikregister 115
Wortschatzregister 117

Erklärung der Lautschrift Umschlagseite 2
Unregelmäßige Verben Umschlagseite 3

1A

A Warm-up

Classroom opinion poll

Each of a group of six students chooses one question from the following list to ask everyone in the class, noting down the answers. Afterwards the "pollsters" report their findings to the class.

Example:

One person has less than four weeks' holiday per year.
Four people have four to five weeks' holiday per year.
Ten have five to six weeks' holiday per year.
Five have more than six weeks' holiday per year.

1. How many weeks' holiday do you have per year?
   ☐ Under 4 weeks. ☐ 4–5 weeks.
   ☐ 5–6 weeks. ☐ Over 6 weeks.
2. Where did you go for your holiday(s) last/this year?
3. How did you travel on your last holiday?
   ☐ Car. ☐ Train. ☐ Plane. ☐ Coach.
   ☐ Ship. ☐ Other.
4. Do you think it's a good idea for married couples to go on separate holidays from time to time?
5. Which do you consider the best place to spend a week's holiday?
   ☐ Family hotel.
   ☐ Furnished holiday flat.
   ☐ Farm.
   ☐ Caravan or tent.
   ☐ Ship.
6. If you wanted to take a holiday job next year, which of the following would be your favourite?
   ☐ Waiter/Waitress in a seaside hotel.
   ☐ Raspberry picking in Britain.
   ☐ Pony-trek leader in Wales.
   ☐ Milkman in a London suburb.

On the camp site: Putting up the tent

4 a) holiday home / cottage
b) , envelope
c) harbour , port
? d) licensed
e) TV-room , TV-lounge
f) proceeds
g) prices , reasonable rates
h) tents

(C) a) want
b) had
c) would
d) will not , won't
e) gave
f) are
g) would
h) will , shall , can

Brief an Hotel schreiben

Texts

1. An after-dinner chat

A You reading the paper?
B Yes . . . The things you can buy for Christmas – solid-gold sunglasses at Harrods for £1,100 – can you imagine anyone buying sunglasses for £1,100?
A If Harrods sell sunglasses at £1,100, there must be people mad enough to buy them.
B And rich enough. We couldn't buy posh sunglasses like that even if we wanted to.
A If I had £1,100 to spare, there'd be a hundred things I'd rather buy than darn sunglasses. We don't have any sunshine anyway. Must be weeks since I last saw the sun. What does the weather forecast say?
B Let me see . . . Ah, here we are: "Rain and snow spreading from the west."
A Blasted winter. I wish we could go away.
B Where to? Rain on the south coast is just as bad as rain in London.
A Worse. – I was thinking of a place like Australia. It must be summer down there now.
B 29 degrees in Sydney, and sunny.
A That's what I thought. I wouldn't mind spending my Christmas holiday on some Australian beach.
B Nor would I, but you know as well as I do that we've got neither the time nor the money to go to Australia just like that. I'll tell you what. Why don't we start planning our next summer holiday?
A You're right. That'll give us something to look forward to as long as there's "rain and snow spreading from the west".

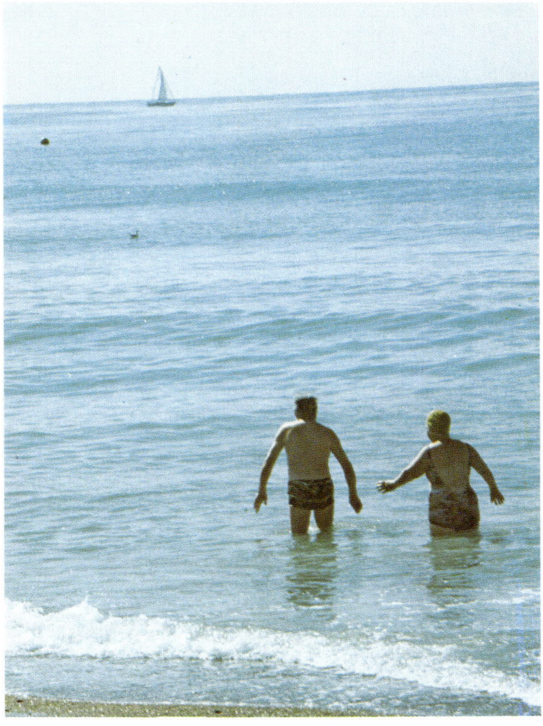

World Weather

(**C** = cloudy, **F** = fair, **R** = rain, **S** = sunny, **Sn** = snow)

		C	F			C	F
Athens	S	14	57	Munich	F	9	48
Berlin	C	9	48	New York	F	0	32
Cairo	S	19	66	Paris	F	10	50
Cape Town	F	22	72	Rome	S	15	59
Dublin	R	11	52	San Francisco	C	9	48
Edinburgh	R	4	39	Stockholm	Sn	0	32
London	F	10	50	Sydney	S	29	84
Majorca	F	17	63	Tokyo	S	9	48
Malta	S	17	63	Vienna	C	4	39
Moscow	C	–19	–2	Zurich	F	7	45

2. Pair work: Checking comprehension

a. What might be the relationship between A and B?
b. At what time of year is the conversation taking place? (Reasons?)
c. What kind of place is Harrods?
d. What does A think of people who buy solid-gold sunglasses?
e. What makes Australia attractive for A and B at this time of year?
f. Why can't A and B go to Australia?

3. [cassette]

Hotels

TORQUAY. Licensed hotel, near harbour and beaches, in own grounds with large heated swimming pool, sauna, games room, TV lounge, excellent food. Car park. Ideal for children, free baby-sitting service. Reasonable rates. Beach House Hotel, 18 Westhill Rd., Torquay.

Caravans

ISLE OF WIGHT. Well-equipped caravan in unspoiled peaceful cottage garden. Ideal sailing, birdwatching, fishing, walks. Tent accepted. For full particulars write to: Mrs I. J. Arnold, 18 St. Paul's Ave., Shanklin.

Time share

FREE HOLIDAYS IN SPAIN! Buy a share in a Spanish holiday home for as little as £350. Enjoy it for 10 years, then take your share of the proceeds of its sale. INTERESTED? Send s.a.e. to F. Powell, 61 Mortimer St., London W1.

Time-sharing:
new development in holidays

Holidays for ever at today's prices!
The wisest investment of a lifetime!

And this is how time-sharing works: You become owner not of a property but of time in that property. You buy a particular week, or weeks, and every year the accommodation is yours for that period.

4. Put in words from the ads on the left

a. They've got a flat in Central London and a little holiday . . . . . with a lovely garden in the country.
b. The sender's address is on the back of the . . . . .
c. Luckily the ship was still in the . . . . . when the storm broke.
d. If you want beer or whisky, we'll have to go to a place that's . . . . .
e. You can watch TV down in the . . . . .
f. The . . . . . of the Christmas bazaar will go to the Dogs Home Battersea.
g. Many hotels offer reduced . . . . . in the autumn, winter, and spring.
h. Most camping areas have sites for caravans and . . . . .

C Insight and practice

Present or past, will or would? Put in verbs where necessary (→ G11)

a. If you . . . . . to know more about the "free holidays in Spain", you must write to the address given in the ad.
b. If we . . . . . a dog, we wouldn't go to England for our holiday.
c. If the pool wasn't heated, we . . . . . probably freeze to death.
d. If we plan our holiday early enough, it . . . . .n't be difficult to find a suitable hotel.
e. If I . . . . . my husband/wife solid-gold sunglasses for Christmas, (s)he'd think I was mad.
f. If all the hotels . . . . . full, we can always sleep in the tent.
g. If I had a few thousand pounds to spare, I . . . . . sail to New York on the *Queen Elizabeth 2*.
h. We . . . . . save two days if we travel by plane.

Transfer

1. Writing to a hotel

You are looking for holiday accommodation in Torquay. Write a letter to the Beach House Hotel (→ advert p. 12), including the following points:

a. Number of persons you require accommodation for.
   Adults – children (what ages)?
b. What period you require accommodation for. (Alternative dates?)
c. Kind of accommodation required (single/double, bathroom/shower, extra bed, etc.).
d. Meals required (Bed and breakfast only? B&B and evening meal? Breakfast, lunch and dinner?)
e. Rates charged per week? Deposit? Reduction for children (ages?)?
f. Brochure available?
g. Other/Special requirements (English summer courses? Tennis court? TV in rooms? Riding, pony trekking? Dog(s)? Etc.)

(Date)

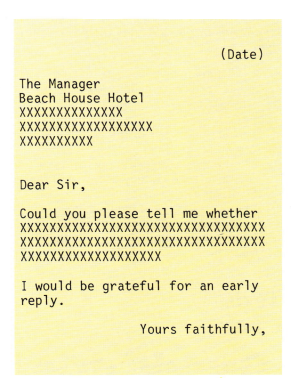

The Manager
Beach House Hotel
XXXXXXXXXXXXXX
XXXXXXXXXXXXXXXXXX
XXXXXXXXXX

Dear Sir,

Could you please tell me whether
XXXXXXXXXXXXXXXXXXXXXXXXXXXXXXXXX
XXXXXXXXXXXXXXXXXXXXXXXXXXXXXXXXX
XXXXXXXXXXXXXXXXXXX

I would be grateful for an early reply.

Yours faithfully,

2. Group work

a. Discuss the pros and cons of time-sharing.
   Pros: "Own" holiday home, cheaper than other holiday accommodation(?), protected against inflation(?), property never empty/unoccupied (burglars!), etc.
   Cons: Tied down to a particular time and place for holiday (unless exchange arrangements are made with other time-sharers), disadvantages of sharing accommodation with up to 51 other people, etc.
b. Discuss the FREE HOLIDAYS IN SPAIN advertisement: Interesting? Make a list of details you would like to know about the property, then write to F. Powell.

2A/B

A Warm-up

Complete these sentences, using either your own words or phrases from the box on the right

a. A policeman who suspects that a motorist has been drinking may ask him to . . .
b. A motorist caught drunk at the wheel may . . .
c. A drug that makes drunk people sober would . . .
d. When police see a car going from side to side on a freeway, they will suspect that the driver . . .
e. When you see a man swaying, it's reasonable for you to think that he . . .
f. When parents drink, it's usually the children who . . .

be a great success
be disqualified from driving
be very successful
blow in the bag
come with him for a blood test
get a jail sentence
get out of the car
give a sample of his breath for testing
has been drinking
have to go to jail
have to pay a fine
is drunk
lose his licence
not be a good thing
sell very well
suffer

B Texts

1.

Drunk driver learns lesson

A MOTORIST who refused to "blow in the bag" when stopped by police has been fined $300 and disqualified from driving for 30 months.

Kevin Smith, 42, self-employed builder, of Stanley St, Melbourne, pleaded not guilty to driving under the influence of alcohol.

Constable David Horne told the court he stopped Smith's car at 8.45 p.m. on May 16 last year because it had been going from side to side on the South Eastern Freeway at Richmond.

When Smith got out of the car, he fell forward and had to be held up. While getting out his driving licence, he swayed, dropping papers and money on the road.

Asked to give a sample of his breath for analysis, Smith refused, saying it was unreasonable to suspect that he was drunk.

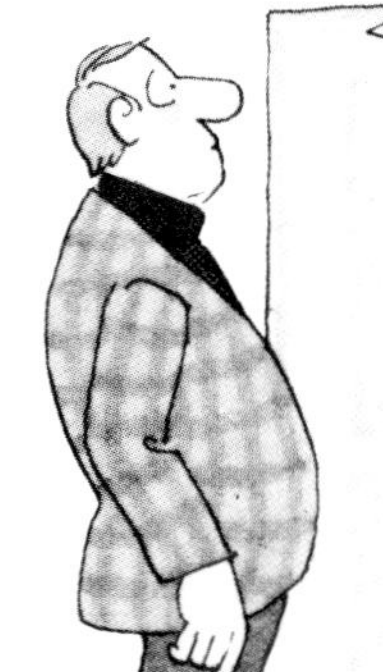

2. Role play: In the Magistrates' Court

Charge: Driving under the influence of alcohol; refusing to give a breath sample for analysis
Mr Smith, defendant: 1st student
Mr Cooke, Mr Smith's lawyer: 2nd student
Mr Skinner, prosecution: 3rd student
Constable Horne, witness: 4th student
Mr Adams, magistrate: 5th student

3. At the pub

Listen to / Read the conversation at the pub, then answer the following:

Which of the three is the least worried about drinking too much?
What might be Tony's occupation?
Explain why Tony might lose his job if his licence is taken away.

GEOFF Nice place this, isn't it?
TONY Yes, and not too crowded either. What will you have, Marge?
MARGE A half of lager, please.
TONY And you, Geoff?
GEOFF I'll have a pint of bitter, please.
Tony gets the drinks at the bar.
TONY Well, here we are. – Cheers!
MARGE AND GEOFF Cheers!
GEOFF Well, let's have another.
TONY No more beer for me, thank you. I'm driving.
GEOFF Not even one for the road?
TONY No, better not. I can't afford to lose my driving licence.
MARGE You're right there, Tony. A colleague of mine was caught when he'd been drinking over the limit. 0.18 per cent, I think.
GEOFF That's quite a lot, isn't it?
MARGE I suppose so. Anyway, he was fined $300, but that didn't bother him too much. What hurt was that his licence was taken away for nine months.
GEOFF Nine months, oh Lord!
TONY That's what I always say. You simply can't risk it. As a salesman you're finished if you lose your licence.

4. Group discussion: Talking about news items

Tragic end of drinking party

DRIVER Kevin McLean killed himself and three other people by driving after drinking 14 pints of beer to celebrate his 21st birthday.

McLean crashed head-on into another car on his way home after the party.

McLean, his two teenage passengers and the driver of the other car were killed outright.

Drink getting cheaper

IN BRITAIN, between 1970 and 1980, real earnings increased and drink became relatively cheaper.

In 1970, the average person had to work 11.4 minutes to earn the price of a pint of beer, as against only 8.4 minutes in 1980.

The drop in the real price of whisky is even greater: four hours' work to earn a bottle of whisky in 1970, one hour 55 minutes in 1980.

Drinking without regret?

AN AMERICAN drug company says it has developed a drug which makes it possible for people to sober up in a hurry.

Drinkers who have had two or three too many will simply put a small amount of the stuff into a glass of water, drink it and wait for their heads to clear.

Tests of the drug were said to have been successful.

a. How could the tragic accident reported above have been prevented?
b. Do you think people drink more, or less, than they did ten years ago?
c. Why do you think people drink more/less than ten years ago?
d. Has drink become relatively more expensive or cheaper in the last ten years? Is that a good thing?
e. What is the new drug developed in the U.S. supposed to do? Do you think such a drug would be a good thing?

2B

5. [cassette symbol]

Dear Carol...  **LETTERS**

Parents' drinking problem worries 12-year-old

I'M A 12-YEAR-OLD girl with a problem I can't talk to anybody about, and it's getting worse.

I'm the oldest of three children. We live in a nice neighbourhood. We aren't poor and we aren't rich. Mum works part-time as a nurse, and Dad works every day except weekends – and that's when the trouble starts. Dad starts drinking on Friday night and he stays drunk all weekend.

When he's drunk he gets nasty to Mum, and there's so much shouting and fighting I'm afraid the neighbours will hear it.

Now Mum has started to drink with him, and she even drinks during the daytime when she's at home. When Dad comes home and she's been drinking, they have a big fight. I'm afraid they're going to get divorced. I'm ashamed to have my friends over, and I don't want to go anywhere when my parents are drinking because I worry about my brother, who is 9, and my sister, who is 6.

What can I do? Don't tell me to try to talk some sense into them. Who would listen to a 12-year-old kid?

6. Comprehension, discussion and letter writing

The above letter appeared on a newspaper's "personal problem page".

a. Make sure you've got all the facts right:
   The girl: Age? Brothers and sisters?
   Her parents: Father's, mother's job?
   The family's situation.
   The girl's problem: Father, mother, the parents' marriage?
   Why doesn't the girl talk to anybody about her problem?
   Why doesn't she have friends over, or go out?
   Why doesn't she try to talk some sense into her parents?

b. Discuss possible ways of helping the girl and her parents.

c. You are "Carol". Write a letter in answer to the girl's letter.

Insight and practice

C

Pair work: How long . . .? (→ G10)

A	The bus drivers are on strike. (three days)
B	Oh, are they? How long have they been on strike?
A	I think they've been on strike for three days now.

A	They've got a diesel now. (the beginning of the year)
B	Oh, have they? How long have they had it?
A	I think they've had it since the beginning of the year.

a. Susan is married. (about a year)
b. The house next to ours is unoccupied. (last Christmas)
c. Dr Taylor is on holiday. (the beginning of the school holidays)
d. That car is following us. (about five minutes)
e. The children are playing. (about two hours)
f. Helen's working for a drug company in California now. (about six months)
g. The Browns have a holiday flat on the south coast. (about two years)
h. Aunt Joan has a dog now. (Uncle Fred died)

Transfer

D

1. Pair work: Conditional sentences (→ G11)

What would happen if there were jail sentences for drink-drivers?
Motorists would probably drink less.
There would probably be fewer drink-driving accidents.

What would happen if there were drugs that made drinkers sober?
What would happen if the price of alcohol increased at the same rate as average earnings?
What would happen if the price of a pint of bitter was £2?
What would happen if the blood-alcohol limit was lowered to .05 per cent?
What would happen if the manufacture or sale of alcoholic drinks was completely forbidden in this country?

2. Pair work: Try to talk sense into your partner

a. Your partner has had three halves of bitter and a Scotch and wants to go on drinking though (s)he is driving.
b. Your partner is swaying but wants to drive home himself/herself.
c. Your partner boasts (s)he can drink any-one under the table.
d. Your partner goes out drinking every weekend leaving his/her family alone.

3A/B

A Warm-up

Pair work (→ G18)

A says: I can type. *B says:* I can type too. *(Or:)* So can I. *(Or otherwise:)* 'I 'can't.	*A says:* I speak French. *B says:* I speak French too. *(Or:)* So do I. *(Or otherwise:)* 'I 'don't.
A says: I can't type. *B says:* I can't type either. *(Or:)* Nor can I. *(Or otherwise:)* 'I 'can.	*A says:* I don't speak French. *B says:* I don't speak French either. *(Or:)* Nor do I. *(Or otherwise:)* 'I 'do.

Go on with:

a. I can('t) sing very well.
b. I (don't) work in . . .
c. I can('t) sew.
d. I (don't) smoke.
e. I'm (not) married.
f. I (don't) like beer.
g. I'm (not) good at . . .
h. I've / I haven't got a dog.
i. I (don't) make my own clothes.
j. I've / I haven't got a car.
k. I've (never) been to America.
Etc.

B Texts

1. On the ball from nine to five

Janet and Brenda work in a tennis-ball factory. Seven hours a day, five days a week, forty-nine weeks a year they go through the same routine:
Janet puts a newly made ball in a metal claw above her head, pulls a string and lets the ball drop.
Brenda, sitting alongside, looks into a mirror which has two pieces of tape stuck on it horizontally 54 inches and 58 inches above the floor. She checks that the ball bounces to a point between the two lines. Otherwise it must not be passed for sale.
Janet and Brenda inspect every ball that leaves the factory – millions of them each year.

2. Working while others sleep

Jack's is a nine-to-five job all right but one with a difference. His working "day" in a newspaper printing shop starts at 9 p.m. and ends just after 5 a.m.

Jack is 49 years old and married with three children. He's been working nights for 26 years. "It's honestly never worried me," he says. "You get used to it. I go to sleep when I'm tired and get up when I wake up. However, I make a point of being up to have breakfast with my children before they go to school."

SHORT OF CASH
AND WILLING TO WORK?

Whether you're skilled or unskilled, young or old, male or female, white or coloured, we'll probably have a job for you.
Send your details, skills and s.a.e. to:

Jobs Unlimited
36 Maddox Street · London W1

3. Making her own way

When 16-year-old Tracey left school, she knew what she wanted to be: a vet's assistant. She tried the Jobcentre and wrote to every vet in the area, but without success. There were no jobs for vets' assistants and there weren't any other jobs either. She had just two choices: to join the dole queue or make her own way by using her talents.

She had taken a course in dress designing at school and was already making her own clothes. When her friends asked her to make their dresses, she realized that might be a way of earning a living.

With her mother's sewing machine and remnants of material picked up cheaply at local markets, she worked hard every day making the kind of clothes that appeal to disco-dancing youngsters at prices they can afford.

It was heavy going at first, but her efforts began to pay off when she put on a fashion show at a local disco, using her friends as models.

4. Willing to do anything

Dear Jobs Unlimited,

I'm 22 years old, female, German, single, and looking for part-time work, preferably mornings.

I could type (two fingers), do translations, answer the phone, teach German, sell, prepare simple meals, sew, clean, wash cars, baby-sit, look after kids or someone who's lonely, take someone's dog for a walk, sing (German folk songs), or act (I've worked as an extra).

I'm tidy, prepared to work hard, quick to learn, and reasonably good-looking.

I'm running out of money, so if you've got a job for me, please do let me know without delay.

Yours truly,

Daniela Schreiber

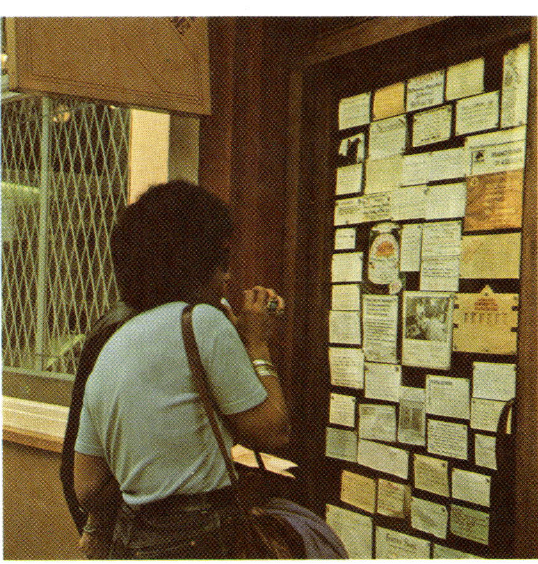

5. Questions on the texts

a. Take a tennis ball, then together with a partner demonstrate Janet's and Brenda's job to the class, explaining what you're doing.
b. Describe Jack's day. Do you think he sleeps 7–8 hours a day, as "normal" people do?
c. Why do you think Tracey's business was "heavy going" at first?
d. What kind of jobs do you think an agency like Jobs Unlimited has to offer?
e. As far as you can see from Daniela's letter, do you think she's been trained for any particular occupation?

6. Put in words from the texts

a. The cat had a mouse in its . . . . .
b. Paris is one of the world's centres for fashion . . . . .
c. Like many other famous actresses and actors, Sophia Loren began her acting career as an . . . . .
d. Old people living alone are often . . . . .
e. Newspapers are usually . . . . . at night.
f. A lathe operator is a . . . . . worker.
g. I need some . . . . . to tie this parcel up.
h. The whole concert was recorded on . . . . .
i. When our dog was ill, we took him to the . . . . .

C

He makes a point of going away in August

Insight and practice

1. Make a point of + -ing (→ G20)

I'm up to have breakfast with my children before they go to school. I make a point of being up to have breakfast with my children before they go to school.

Expand the following sentences

a. I'm at my desk by half past eight.
b. We check every ball that leaves the factory.
c. I answer every letter the day it arrives.
d. I wash my car once a week.
e. I take my dog for a long walk in the park every day.
f. I read the local paper every day.
g. I go to the dentist every six months.
h. He said as little as possible at the meeting.

2. Preposition + -ing (→ G20)

You must try to make your own way . . . . . your talents.
You must try to make your own way by using your talents.

Complete the following sentences

a. Making dresses might be a way . . . . . a living.
b. In the magistrates' court he pleaded guilty . . . . . a car with a blood-alcohol content of 0.18 per cent.
c. She has a talent . . . . . dresses.
d. You can call the operator . . . . . 999.
e. He never does anything important . . . . . his horoscope first.
f. Many thanks . . . . . after the kids.
g. We have pleasure . . . . . your reservation of one single room with a private bath.
h. We're looking forward . . . . . you in the summer.
i. This bag is useful . . . . . things bought on a trip.
j. Instead . . . . . TV you should read a good book.

Transfer

D

a. Remember Janet and Brenda, who work in the tennis-ball factory?
Do you think they're happy checking tennis balls day in, day out?
How do you think they feel when they watch the Wimbledon tennis on TV and see "their" balls being used by the tennis stars?

b. Consider Jack, who's been working nights for 26 years.
Would you like to work at night as he does? (Why or why not?)
Talk about yourself:
If I had to work at night, I'd . . .
c. And Tracey, the girl who wanted to be a vet's assistant:
Try to describe what kind of person she is.
What might other youngsters have done in her position?
d. Finally the German girl in London, Daniela Schreiber.
Compare her with Tracey. In what ways are the two girls similar?
If you were in Daniela's position, on your own in London and running out of money, what would you do?
e. You are in London and you are short of cash. You have to earn money if you want to stay alive. Write to Jobs Unlimited, mentioning all your skills and talents, anything that you might do and get paid for.

Time for a break 1

TAG QUESTION MAMBO

↱	The accident could have been prevented,	You simply can't risk it,	She bought it at Harrods,	does she?
You wouldn't mind going away,	You didn't pay a deposit,	isn't it?	can you?	is it?
They live in Dallas,	That's a good idea,	aren't you?	don't they?	would you?
The south coast isn't any better,	He hasn't been drinking,	isn't he?	hasn't it?	aren't they?
Dr Taylor's on holiday,	The hotel's got a sauna,	do you?	were you?	doesn't she
↳	They won't send him to jail,	Things are getting worse,	You're going to your English class,	That'll give something look forwar to,

TAG QUESTION MAMBO

e reads the ily Mail,	You don't want to take a holiday job,	That's what you thought,	The new drug's selling very well,	
you?	didn't she?	hasn't she?	Your wife doesn't smoke,	They're still on holiday,
ldn't it?	won't it?	isn't she?	You weren't thinking of a man like Bert,	Nice place this,
't we?	will they?	isn't there?	She's really got talent,	There's a heated pool,
ld it?	has he?	do they?	Brenda's working nights this week,	A caravan wouldn't be cheaper,
you?	You aren't lonely,	We can watch TV down in the lounge,	They don't read the local paper,	

TAG QUESTION MAMBO

4A

A Warm-up

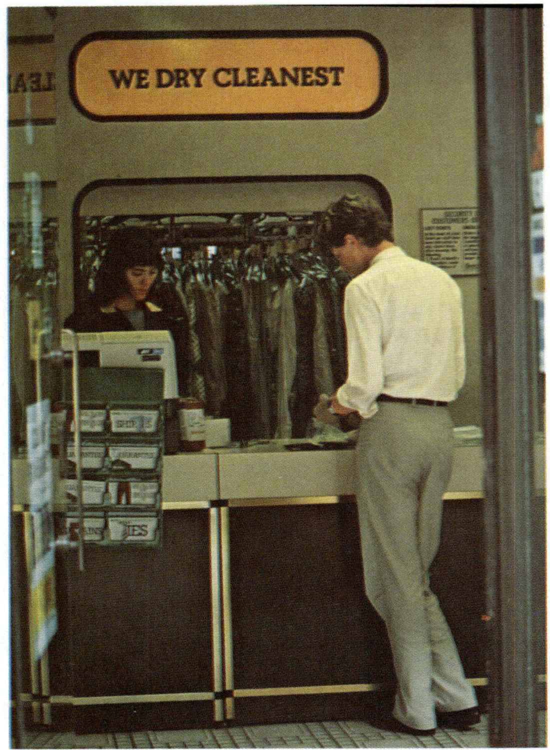

At the dry-cleaner's

1. What would you have done?

a. When Bill used the electric shaver he had bought the day before, it worked for a short time and then stopped. Bill took it back to the store and asked the assistant to exchange it for a new one. The assistant said that was impossible, it would have to be sent in for repair. – Would you have accepted the assistant's answer?

b. No wonder the hamburger Hilary was eating in a snack bar tasted strange somehow. Part of the bun was mouldy, she discovered as she looked more closely. When she showed it to an attendant, he just shrugged and offered her a replacement. – Would that have satisfied you if you had been in Hilary's position?

2. Role play: Making a complaint

Your floor-length curtains were supposed to have been dry-cleaned, but on collecting them at the shop, you find that they have been washed instead and are now about 20 inches shorter than before.
Two students act the scene out, student A being the customer, and student B the assistant in the cleaner's shop.

Look what's happened to . . . You've ruined . . . . . . your fault . . . I must insist . . .	I'm terribly sorry but . . . You said . . . . . . replace the curtains . . .

The other students watch the scene, then say what they would have done.

If I'd been the customer/assistant, I would (not) have said/asked/demanded/insisted/ refused/offered/replaced . . .

Text

1. [cassette symbol]

On the art of complaining

"IF YOU have a complaint," says psychologist Mark Davies, "you've got to be aggressive to get results."

When his daughter's newly bought jeans split at the seams the first time she wore them, his wife took them back at a quiet time and politely pointed out the fault. The assistant just shrugged his shoulders. "Sorry, there's nothing we can do."

To demonstrate his method to his wife and daughter, Mr Davies went back to the store when it was most crowded, stood on a chair and shouted: "Who sold my daughter this rubbish?" Half a minute later the girl had a new pair of jeans.

"Always choose the busiest time to complain," says Mr Davies. "Speak loudly to show you mean business. Never accept invitations to 'come into the office' or 'wait until later'."

When consumer-protection specialist Mike Edwards recently arrived at a Canadian hotel, he was told that his reservation had been cancelled by mistake and now – sorry! – they were fully booked. "I'll give you three minutes to find me a room," Mr Edwards told the manager, "then I'm going to undress in the lobby, put on my pyjamas and go to sleep on one of the sofas." He immediately got a room.

When big firms or organizations make mistakes, you'll hardly ever find an employee who says: "Sorry, my fault, I'll sort it out straight away." The cause of the trouble is always something beyond the control of the person you're dealing with: the weather, the breakdown of a lorry or computer, the rail strike, the flu, the situation in the Middle East.

The advice given by people successful at complaining is: "Never show any interest or sympathy for such explanations, don't even listen to them, interrupt your opponent right at the beginning, attack him by saying: "I don't care whose fault it is. I'm holding you responsible, and if you don't get this sorted out by next Monday, I'll bring it to the attention of your head office."

2. If . . . – Try to complete these sentences

a. If Mrs Davies had been more aggressive, the assistant would probably . . .
b. If Mr Davies had accepted an invitation to go into the manager's office, he would probably . . .
c. If Mr Edwards had not threatened to cause trouble . . .
d. If I had been in Mr Davies' position, I would (not) have . . .
e. If I had been in Mr Edwards' position, I . . .
f. If I had been the hotel manager, and Mr Edwards had threatened to sleep in the hotel lounge, I . . .
g. If I had been a shop assistant in the store when Mr(s) Davies came in, I . . .

"Oh no, sir, you can't just buy a new strap. You have to have the whole watch."

4C

C Insight and practice

1. Should(n't) have + past participle (→ G15)

The cleaners shouldn't have washed the curtain. Mrs Davies should have been more aggressive.

Now complete the following sentences

a. Bill's electric shaver . . .
b. The cleaners . . .
c. The girl's new jeans . . .
d. The Canadian hotel . . .
e. The employee who made the mistake . . .
f. Hilary's hamburger . . .

2. Relative clauses (→ G7)

Expand the sentences by adding relative clauses to the underlined nouns

The woman was very polite.		
The woman	who complained about the jeans I complained to about the jeans she asked we discussed the matter with whose daughter had bought the jeans	was very polite.

a. The customer was very aggressive.
b. The shaver didn't work.
c. The store refused to exchange it for a new one.
d. The hamburger tasted strange.
e. The assistant just shrugged his shoulders.
f. The curtains are now 20 inches shorter than before.
g. The jeans split at the seams.
h. The method is very successful.
i. The reservation has been cancelled.
j. The advice is very good.
k. The explanation did not satisfy me.

3. Conditional sentences (→ G11)

Type 1: If he speaks loudly, people will listen to him.
Type 2: If he spoke loudly, people would listen to him.
Type 3: If he had spoken loudly, people would have listened to him.

Make sentences, using the three types of conditional sentences as you think fit

a. if you / drive / with a blood-alcohol content of 0.2 per cent / you / lose / your licence
b. if Spain / win / the 1982 World Cup / everybody / be / surprised
c. if people / drive / more carefully / there / be / fewer accidents
d. if Tracey / find / a job as a vet's assistant / she / not become / a dress designer
e. if my English / be / better / I / become / an English teacher
f. if the weather / not be / so terrible / they / enjoy / their last holiday more
g. if I / be / a cat / I / only kill / mice, not birds
h. if the old man's dog / not die / he / not be / so lonely
i. if you / not drive / more carefully / you / have / an accident one day
j. if he / not drink / so much / he / not die / so young

Transfer

D

Role play: Complaining by letter or phone

You've just come back from a two-week package holiday in Spain which the travel firm's brochure had described as "the holiday of a lifetime". This is what you found instead:

Hotel uncompleted: noise from building work, dust, inconvenience. No swimming pool. Room overlooking busy street, no bath – only shower, often without hot water. Food awful. Beach dirty (building rubble, empty plastic bottles and tins). Hardly got any sleep (two night clubs, one disco just a stone's throw from your bedroom window). Prices exorbitant: £1 for a Coke, £2 for an ice cream. Lousy service.

Write a letter to the Managing Director of the tour operators: Perfect Holidays Ltd, 98 Great Portland St, London W1. – Alternatively, ring the Managing Director (another student) to complain.

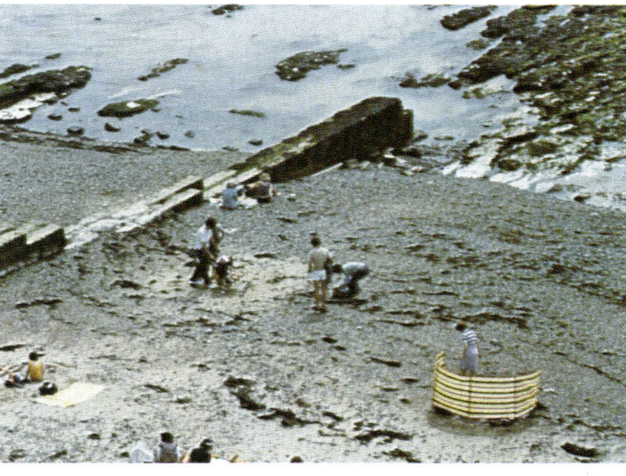

5A/B

A Warm-up

Letters, words, and a proverb

The answers to the following clues (all of them single words) are to be formed from the letters in the square. (The number of letters in each answer is given in brackets.)
Cross off the letters of each word found. The remaining letters, when put in the right order, are a two-word English proverb.

1. A public place where young people dance to recorded pop music. (5) D . . .
2. Useless things that have been, or are to be, thrown away. (7) R . . .
3. A suit you wear in bed, consisting of trousers and a jacket. (7) P . . .
4. A piece of hanging cloth that can be drawn across a window to shut the light out. (7) C . . .
5. A sort of book giving information about holidays, products, etc. (8) B . . .
6. Trousers made of strong, usually blue, cotton cloth. (5) J . . .
7. The flat land next to the sea, covered with sand or small stones. (5) B . . .
8. Someone who works for wages or a salary. (8) E . . .
9. A person who eats, uses, buys things, opposite of the producer. (8) C . . .
10. Someone who has studied the science of the human mind and the way it works; a person who knows a great deal about human nature. (12) P . . .

A	A	A	A	A	B	B	B	B
C	C	C	C	C	C	D	E	E
E	E	E	E	E	E	E	F	G
H	H	H	H	I	I	I	I	I
I	J	J	L	L	L	M	M	M
M	N	N	N	O	O	O	O	O
O	P	P	P	R	R	R	R	R
S	S	S	S	S	S	S	S	T
T	T	U	U	U	U	Y	Y	Y

B Text

1. The first time you listen to / read the following conversation, try to find out the answers to the following questions:

> What day of the week did the raid take place?
> What day was the theft discovered?
> What day is the conversation between A and B taking place?

The Hatton Garden bank raid

A Did you hear about that bank raid in the City today?
B Another bank raid? There have been so many recently, they're no longer news.
A But this one is news. They said it could be the biggest bank raid ever.
B How's that? I thought banks didn't have all that much cash these days. I mean, people usually pay by cheque or they transfer money from one account to another, don't they, so there oughtn't to be too much cash lying around in the banks.

A I know, but in this case the thieves got into the strongroom of the bank and stole what was in the safe-deposit boxes. They cleaned out over a hundred of them. The bank officials say they may have got away with tens of millions of pounds.

B Good heavens! There must have been plenty of valuable things in those boxes.

A Jewels, gold, and cash. The bank is right opposite Hatton Garden.

B Hatton Garden? That's a street, isn't it?

A Yes, and one of the centres of the international diamond trade. Some of the biggest dealers were among the customers of the bank that was raided.

B A hundred boxes full of jewels, gold and money – just imagine! The robbers must have been very clever. Did they just walk into the bank, point a gun at somebody and say: "Open the strongroom, then get out of the way"?

A No, apparently the thieves came on Sunday. They unlocked the bank's front door and walked in.

B Isn't that strange?

A Yes it is, isn't it? It appears they also had a key for the strongroom.

B A smooth professional job.

A Yes, obviously. No one noticed the theft until this morning.

B You mean it took them two days to discover that they'd been robbed?

A Exactly that. The bank people tried to open the door of the strongroom yesterday morning, and when they couldn't, they thought the lock was just jammed.

B They didn't suspect anything?

A No, not then. They called in some engineers and locksmiths but all their efforts to open the lock failed. At long last they made the decision to cut through the wall beside the doors.

B That must have been a hell of a job!

A It took them till this morning. It was only then that they discovered that the boxes had been forced open and all the valuables stolen.

B Good Lord! But surely a bank like that ought to have an alarm system, what about that?

A The police say there was an alarm on Sunday morning. They went to check but found nothing wrong, so they thought it had been a false alarm.

B And how much did you say was missing? Millions?

A Possibly tens of millions. No one knows the exact amount, perhaps they never will. You see, the safe-deposit boxes are opened and locked only by the customers, so they alone know what's in them.

B But then, how can one prove one's loss to the insurance people?

A One can't, and that's why it seems things held in a safe-deposit box are not insured. At least, that's what the reporter said.

5B/C

"Head Office have promised us a closed-circuit television by next year."

2. Pair work: Making sure of the facts

a. What's Hatton Garden?
b. What made the bank opposite Hatton Garden particularly "attractive" to robbers?
c. What did the robbers steal?
d. Why was the theft discovered so late?
e. Did the bank's alarm system work?
f. Why didn't the bank know exactly how much was stolen?

C Insight and practice

1. Must/Should/. . . have + past participle (→ G15)

Make statements about the Hatton Garden bank raid, using the structure *could/may/must/ . . . have been/had/got/. . .*

The robbers must have been very clever. The keys should have been kept in a safer place. *Etc.*				
It The thieves The robbers They The theft The bank (people) The valuables The police The keys The contents of the safe-deposit boxes There	can('t) could(n't) may (not) might(n't) must should(n't) ought(n't) to	have	(be) (come) (get) (have) (know) (protect) (take)	one of the biggest bank raids ever. away with tens of millions of pounds. plenty of jewels, gold, and cash in the boxes. what was in the safe-deposit boxes. amateurs/professionals. on Sunday. keys to the bank's doors. in through the front door. kept in a safer place. discovered earlier. protected more carefully. the strongroom more carefully. employees of the bank. the alarm more seriously. very clever/careful/careless.

2. If . . . – Complete these sentences (→ G11)

If the robbers hadn't had keys . . . (not get into the strongroom)
If the robbers hadn't had keys, they wouldn't/couldn't/mightn't have got into the strongroom.

a. If the customers of the bank hadn't been diamond dealers . . . (not be so many jewels in the safe-deposit boxes)
b. If the alarm had been taken more seriously . . . (the police catch the robbers / the robbery be discovered much earlier)
c. If the lock of the strongroom door hadn't been jammed . . . (the bank staff discover the robbery much earlier)
d. If the contents of the safe-deposit boxes had been insured . . . (the insurance company be ruined)
e. If the bank people had been more careful . . . (the robbery not be possible)

D

Transfer

1. Role play: Interviewing the bank manager

The robbery at the bank opposite Hatton Garden was discovered only a short time ago. A reporter (student A) asks the bank manager (student B) about details of the robbery.
(Alternatively, there could be a press conference: Several reporters [students] ask the bank manager questions.)

Things stolen?
When? Where? How?
Why discovered so late?
Insured?
Who responsible?
Etc.

2. Writing a news story

Would you like to try your hand at writing a news story about the Hatton Garden bank raid? If so, you may or may not want to use the outline on the right.

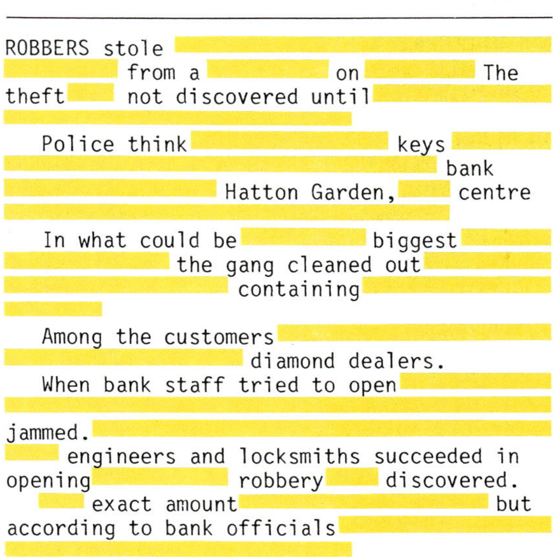

ROBBERS stole ______ from a ______ on ______ The theft ______ not discovered until ______

Police think ______ keys ______ bank ______ Hatton Garden, ______ centre ______

In what could be ______ biggest ______ the gang cleaned out ______ containing ______

Among the customers ______ diamond dealers.
When bank staff tried to open ______ jammed. ______ engineers and locksmiths succeeded in opening ______ robbery ______ discovered. ______ exact amount ______ but according to bank officials ______

6A

A Warm-up

Pair work:
Choices and decisions

a. If you had the choice between trips to Canada, India, or Australia, where would you like to go to? (Reasons?)

b. Look at the temperatures in Alice Springs in the Centre of Australia. In what months do the four seasons fall in Alice Springs? What month would you consider the best time to visit Alice Springs, and why? What clothes would you take along if you were to visit Alice Springs in January/July?

c. Look at the map of time zones in Australia. At what time in this country would you phone someone in Alice Springs if you wanted to catch him/her before going to work/bed?

Australia: Road distances in kilometres

	Adelaide	Alice Springs	Ayers Rock	Darwin	Sydney
Adelaide	□	1690	1739	3212	1431
Alice Springs	1690	□	468	1522	2929
Ayers Rock	1739	468	□	1980	3004
Darwin	3212	1522	1980	□	4060
Sydney	1431	2929	3004	4060	□

Alice Springs: Average temperatures (maximum/minimum)

Jan	Feb	Mar	Apr	May	June	July	Aug	Sept	Oct	Nov	Dec
37	36	33	29	23	20	19	22	26	31	34	35
22	21	18	14	9	6	4	7	10	15	18	20

d. Look at the table of road distances in Australia. What are the longest and shortest distances? How would you travel (air or road?) from Darwin to Adelaide,
a) on business,
b) on holiday?
(Reasons?)

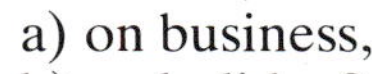

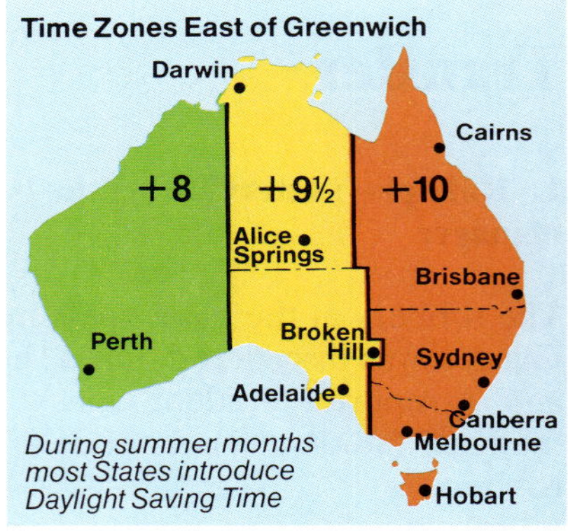

Ayers Rock, one of Australia's most spectacular natural attractions, is a large hill of bare stone in the Red Centre of Australia, 340 kilometres by air southwest of Alice Springs. With a base 8.8 kilometres around, 3.6 kilometres long and 2.4 kilometres wide, the Rock rises 348 metres above the surrounding plains. Ayers Rock is famous for its wonderful, ever-changing colours, especially at sunrise and sunset. Thousands of visitors climb the Rock each year, enter their names in a book at the summit and buy themselves T-shirts with the words "I've climbed Ayers Rock" printed on them.

Texts

1. A letter from Australia

Dear Barbara,

I hope you are well after your holiday in our Northern Territory. My wife and I, and also my brother and his wife, had a very enjoyable time.

It's a pity I had to hurry the last part of the climb down the Rock because our bus was waiting and the driver wanted to show us things of interest at the bottom of the Rock and get us back to one of the motels for our midday meal. I didn't say goodbye and wish you well for the rest of your trip. I hope I congratulated you on a fine effort and a job well done in climbing Ayers Rock.

I suppose you were thinking that chap who took your photo and said he would send you a print has forgotten all about it. But here at last is the photograph that shows you in your moment of glory!

After leaving Ayers Rock we took four days and nights travelling by bus to come down to Adelaide, the capital of South Australia. From there it was only about ten kilometres to our home.

On the way down, there were only twelve passengers on our bus, which was a 44-seater and air-conditioned. The twelve passengers consisted of two Englishwomen, one Scotswoman, a German chap about 35, and eight Australians. We all got to know each other by our first names. It was a delightful trip, and the places we stopped at each night were very pleasant, with good meals and accommodation.

I hope the Australians you met in your travels were kind to you and that you have some happy memories of your holiday in the outback.

With kindest regards, also from my wife,

2. Pair work: Making sure of the facts

a. Where did Donald Webb meet Barbara?
b. What did Donald and Barbara do together?
c. What was Barbara's "moment of glory"?
d. Where is Donald from?
e. Roughly how many kilometres did Donald's bus cover per day on the trip down to Adelaide?
f. Could Barbara be Australian?

Alice Springs, with a population of over 14,000, is at the heart of the Red Centre of Australia, over 1500 kilometres from the nearest State capital.

6B

Mail run from Alice Springs: Once a week a small charter plane delivers mail to cattle stations in the outback as far as 500 kilometres from Alice Springs. Barbara spends a day accompanying the pilot on his run.

On the 1500-kilometre trip from Alice Springs to Darwin Barbara's bus is stopped by a bush fire.

Between the 1860s and the 1920s camels were used for transport between outback stations and the south coast. After lorries and railways had replaced them, the camels were allowed to go wild. There may now be as many as 20,000 wild camels in the Red Centre.

COOBER PEDY

On the way to Ross River Homestead 85 kilometres east of Alice Springs Barbara's bus gets stuck in the sandy road.

After living undisturbed for tens of thousands of years, Australia's Aboriginal people were murdered in large numbers by the white settlers or died of diseases such as smallpox and tuberculosis. Fewer than 50,000 "full-blood" Aboriginals have survived. Robbed of their land, their religion, and their purpose in life, many of them live in poverty and ill health. Rock paintings remind us of their ancient culture.

Insight and practice

C

Expand the sentences meaningfully, as in the examples

John Flynn, the founder of the Royal Flying Doctor Service, lies buried 6 kilometres west of Alice Springs. Nowadays, the doctors seldom fly to the distant cattle and sheep stations any more but mostly diagnose patients and give medical advice by radio.

The people . . . were all very pleasant.
The people she met in the outback . . .
The people who travelled with her . . .
The people staying at the hotel . . .
The people invited to the party were all very pleasant. *Etc.*

a. The day . . . was very hot.
b. The clothes . . . were all too warm.
c. The people . . . entered their names in a book at the summit.
d. The T-shirt . . . had the words "I've climbed Ayers Rock" printed on it.
e. The holiday . . . was extremely enjoyable.
f. The chap . . . promised to send us a print.
g. Here's the photo . . .
h. The photo . . . is very good.
i. The plane . . . was very small.
j. The pilot . . . was very young.

Transfer

D

1. Letter writing

You are Barbara. Answer Donald Webb's letter (→ p. 33), including the following points:
a. Thank you for letter and photograph.
b. Nice meeting Donald and his wife.
c. Your memories of Ayers Rock.
d. Details of your trip through the Northern Territory (see pictures and information on pages 32–35).
e. How you liked Australia and the Australians.

2. Group project: Tourist information

The students work together in groups of 3–4. Each group chooses a sight or tourist attraction in their city/town/village and develops a text to describe it in English and make it interesting for English-speaking visitors. Speakers for the different groups then read the texts out to the class.
(If it is possible to keep the name of the sight a secret, the class could be asked to guess its name.)

Time for a break 2

The Journey to Australia

u are among the first convicts be transported from Britain to stralia by the eleven ling ships of the rst Fleet".

7A/B

A Warm-up

Group work: Examining the news [cassette]

Students, working in groups of 3–4, discuss the following newspaper headlines.
What do they mean?
What's your reaction to them? (Surprised? Shocked? Interested? Pleased?)
Two of the headlines have been made up. Can you spot them?

Bank Robbery Suspect, Age 9, Arrested

● Average Industrial Profits Down to 23.4%

Leonardo Notebook Brings $5 Million

Artificial Skin Reported for Burn Victims

Blinding of Prisoners in India Charged

Composition by Mozart at Age 9 Discovered

Ex-Postal Worker Willed Millions to Blind

Calf Survives With Man-Made Heart

Record $1 Million Paid for a Stamp

First Woman to Row in Oxford's Boat

Oldest American Dies Aged 137

First Sun-Powered Airplane Crosses Channel

B

Text

1. A modern dilemma [cassette]

A It looks as if a nuclear war wouldn't have to be all that terrible.
B Are you mad?
A No, it's this article here in the newspaper. The Post Office say they've now got emergency plans for delivering the mail even after a nuclear attack.
B Is that supposed to mean there'll be postmen struggling through the rubble and radiation trying to find a letter box to put a mail-order catalogue in?
A They say there'll be a place in each district where Post Office staff can find shelter. Probably some sort of cellar or bunker. They keep food there, medical supplies, even change-of-address forms.

B Change-of-address forms? There won't be any addresses left after a nuclear attack, will there? Everything will be destroyed – houses, blocks, streets, the lot. What kind of fool has thought up all that nonsense?
A It seems there's been a whole team of officials at work, and they've produced a thick book telling people how the postal service will continue when the mushroom cloud has cleared.
B If it's not some sort of black humour, it's downright criminal.
C Criminal? What do you mean by that?
B Well, it might lead people to believe you can fight a nuclear war and survive it, even win it.
C That's what some politicians are saying anyway. They tell you if there's a nuclear war, it'll do more damage to the enemy than to your own country.
D Yes, but you can't be more than dead, can you? That's why all that talk about overkill is just a load of rubbish.
B Quite. The whole idea of nuclear deterrence just won't work in the long run.
C Wait a minute, surely it's because of the nuclear balance between the superpowers that we've had such a long period of peace . . .
D . . . and all the time the nuclear stockpiles have been getting bigger and bigger. More and more nations are getting nuclear weapons. What if some smaller country starts using them in a regional war, or someone pushes the button by mistake?
B Yes. As far as I can see, there's only one way to prevent a nuclear holocaust in the long run, and that's a total ban on nuclear weapons.
D So what we need is an agreement between the superpowers, but how's that to be brought about as long as there isn't a minimum of trust and goodwill between them?

2. Find words in 7B1 to complete the following sentences

a. There's an interesting . . . . . on nuclear power plants in today's paper.
b. The opposite of war is . . . . .
c. After the explosion, there was nothing left of the house but . . . . .
d. When the storm broke, everybody ran for . . . . .
e. "Rubbish" is another word for "humbug" or . . . . .
f. The storm did a lot of . . . . .
g. If you talk such nonsense, they'll think you're . . . . .
h. He was extremely lucky to . . . . . the crash.
i. People don't seem to have much . . . . . in the Government's ability to solve these problems.
j. Nuclear war must be . . . . . at all costs.
k. Has there ever been a time when the mail was also . . . . . on Sundays?
l. You start the machine by . . . . . this button here.
m. Some people managed to leave the burning theatre by the . . . . . exit.

Balance of power

3. Find words in 7B1 which mean about the same as the underlined expressions in the following sentences

a. Scientists are discussing the pros and cons of <u>atomic</u> energy.
b. Don't listen to him. He's talking <u>rubbish</u>.
c. Petrol can be <u>made</u> from coal.
d. He's written a <u>fat</u> book on the history of Australia.
e. Will you <u>go on</u> playing after lunch?
f. <u>An increasing number of</u> people are beginning to think there should be a total ban on nuclear weapons.

C Insight and practice

1. Singular or plural? Please complete (→ G2)

a. The people at the meeting yesterday ..... very much against the plan.
b. The contents of the safe-deposit box ..... not insured.
c. The Post Office now ..... plans for delivering the mail after a nuclear attack.
d. The police now ..... the robbers had a key for the strongroom.
e. Fifty dollars ..... a lot of money if you're out of work.
f. Our family ..... here for hundreds of years.
g. The United States ..... an independent nation for over 200 years.
h. In a way, the United Nations ..... a mirror of the world we live in.
i. Some of our staff ..... with us for over twenty years.
j. The fighting around the airport continued for a week before the enemy ..... defeated.
k. Cambridge ..... won the Boat Race more often than Oxford.
l. Four miles ..... too far to walk tonight.
m. The cattle ..... hungry and thirsty.
n. ..... the news last night simply awful?

Liverpool win European Cup

England take 3-1 lead

New Zealand defeat Wales by 23–3

Italy regain World Cup after 44 years

2. Make statements using the time phrase "for . . . years (now)" (→ G10)

have peace We've had peace for (about) 40 years now.
live here I've been living here for 15 years now.

a. this country – have a democratic government
b. have my/his/her driving licence
c. have our dog / car / colour TV / house
d. learn English
e. play football/tennis/chess/. . .
f. know Peter/Ruth/. . .
g. the . . . Party – be in power
h. the Aboriginals – be in Australia
i. Shakespeare – be dead

3. Talk about developments during the last year as you see them (→ G10)

Prices have gone up/down.
The economic situation has improved.

a. The number of unemployed (rise/fall).
b. The rate of inflation (go) up/down.
c. There (be) no/some major strikes.
d. Interest rates (rise/fall).
e. International relations (improve / get worse).
f. Air and water pollution (get) worse/better.
g. The Government (do) a good/bad job.
h. The quality of life ([not] improve).

War has become a luxury which only the small nations can afford. (Hannah Arendt, 1971)

Transfer

D

Pair work: Agreeing or disagreeing with your partner

a. Your partner is a Post Office official who tells you the Post Office have developed emergency plans to make sure the mail can be delivered even after a nuclear attack. Tell him/her what you think of the idea.
b. Your partner says: "Our only chance to prevent nuclear war is to have more and better nuclear weapons than the other side." Say you agree or disagree with him/her, and why.
c. Discuss this point made by your partner: "We must start by destroying our nuclear stockpiles, then the other side will do the same and there'll be no danger of nuclear war."

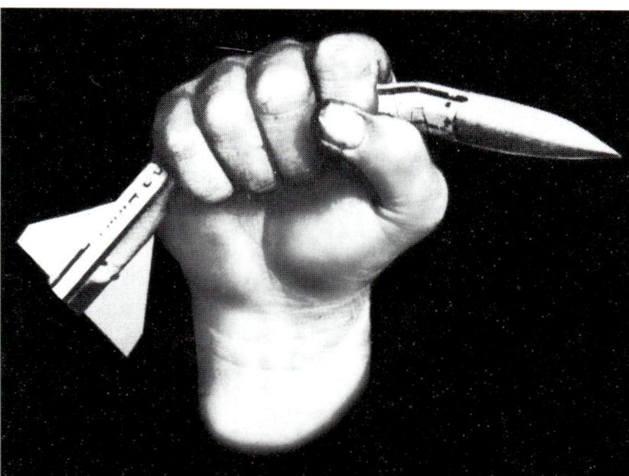

From a CND brochure (Campaign for Nuclear Disarmament)

d. "If there's a nuclear balance between the superpowers, there's not much danger of a nuclear war being started." React to this point made by your partner.
e. At a party someone suggests it might be a good idea to build a private atomic bunker. Say what you think of the idea.

8 A/B

A Warm-up

Pair work: Finding the right class

Student A wants to take an English course at a language school. Student B is a teacher who interviews A to find the right class for him/her.

a. Where did you learn your English?
   Secondary school? Evening classes?
   Other school/college?
   For how many years?
   For how many hours a week?
b. Have you ever been to an English-speaking country?
   If so: When? Where? How long? Did you improve your English?
c. What do you want to use your English for?
d. Which is the most important for you:
   Reading/Writing?
   Listening/Speaking?
   Ability to translate/interpret?
   Understanding grammar?
e. What kind of course would you like to take?
   Normal/Intensive?
   Two/Four/Six or more hours a week?
f. How much homework can you do?

B Texts

1. [cassette symbol]

Professor says "never too old to learn"

"IT IS wrong to believe that the ability to learn something new declines with age," says Professor James Coleman, the well-known psychologist. "The brain goes on functioning normally into the latest years, provided it is kept in practice. As long as you stay active, you need not worry about losing your ability to learn."

According to Professor Coleman, groups of retired men and women aged 60 or more had learnt to speak a foreign language or play a musical instrument. Tests had shown that the elderly citizens achieved the same rate of progress as secondary-school children or young people in their twenties and thirties.

2. Complete the following in your own words

Many people believe that learning becomes more difficult . . . but this is . . .
If you keep in practice . . .
Someone who has kept his mind active all his life . . .
Elderly citizens learning to speak a foreign language . . .

3. A circular letter

St James's School of English
37 St James's Street
London SW1A 1HG
Phone: 01-839 4560

24th January, 1983

Dear Reader,

I know you can read English, but can you speak it as fluently as you would like? Do you understand an American as easily as someone from Britain? Are your children as good at English as they need to be in this modern world?

However well you, or your children, were taught at school, it is obvious that you can't achieve real fluency in English unless you spend some time in an English-speaking country.

Given some knowledge of English to begin with, it is not too difficult a task to become fluent, and we at St James's School have the know-how and experience to help you do it. We have been teaching English as a foreign language for 20 years, to a total of over 30,000 students from overseas. The children of some of our early pupils are already coming back to us!

Here are some of the features that have made St James's School particularly successful at teaching English to foreigners:

* Small classes at 11 different levels, from Elementary to Very Advanced.
* Special courses in commercial and technical English.
* Special entrance test to make sure students are placed in the right class.
* Well-trained, experienced teachers from different parts of the English-speaking world, some of them specialists in commercial or technical English.
* Intensive teaching supported by the very latest audio and visual equipment.
* Accommodation with carefully chosen English families.
* Sightseeing tours, excursions, and parties organized by the School.

I enclose a brochure providing more information about us and look forward to welcoming you or your children - or indeed the whole family! - to St James's School this year.

Yours sincerely,

Hilary Franklin

Hilary Franklin
Principal

4. Comprehension and extension

a. 8B3 is a circular letter sent to thousands of people. Where do you think the school got the addresses from? How does the writer know the person who receives the letter "can read English"?

b. What does the writer say you must do to become really fluent in English? Do you agree?

c. The letter lists a number of arguments in favour of the school. Which of them do you consider particularly important, and why?

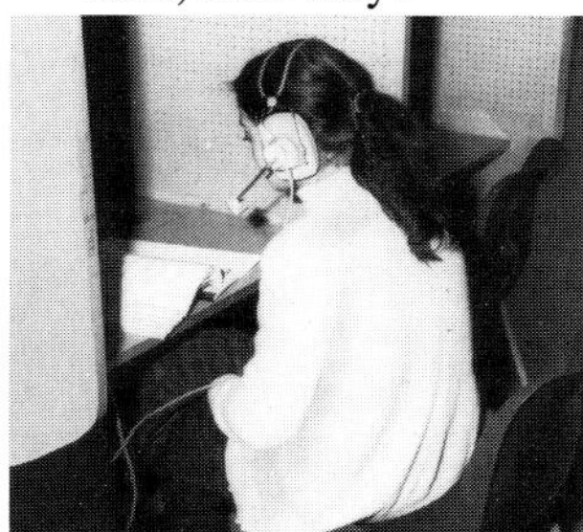

d. You are thinking of spending your next summer holiday in England to improve your English. Could St James's School be the right school for you? Why (not)?

e. St James's School is in London. Would you prefer a school at the seaside? (Reasons?)

8C

C Insight and practice

1. Change the following sentences so that the underlined adjectives become adverbs

His English is fluent. He speaks English fluently.

a. It was obvious that he didn't want to show it to us.
b. He was very careful in his work.
c. Her son is very good at English.
d. The news gave her a terrible shock.
e. He was lucky not to break his leg.
f. The bank is sure to have an alarm system.
g. It's not usual for our customers to pay with travellers' cheques.
h. It would have been easy for the thieves to get into the strongroom.
i. Tests of the drug are said to have been successful.
j. When she took a close look at the bun, she discovered that it was mouldy.

2. Infinitive, -ing form, or preposition + -ing form? (→ G19, G20)

Infinitive:	I'd like **to know** what she thinks of the idea.
-ing form:	I wouldn't enjoy **spending** the evenings at a gambling casino.
Preposition + -ing form:	There are several ways **of solving** the problem.

a. The shop has offered (reduce) the price. **b.** Would you mind (wait) till Mr Brown is back? **c.** It shouldn't be too difficult (find) a suitable hotel. **d.** That's not a nice way (earn) a living. **e.** She's very good (get) people to talk. **f.** Why didn't you accept their invitation (stay) with them? **g.** She doesn't want to go on (live) there after all that's happened. **h.** Be careful with these papers – we can't afford (lose) them. **i.** I think I could never get used (work) at night. **j.** Look – it's started (rain). **k.** What plans does the new Government have (solve) the unemployment problem? **l.** I'm afraid I'm not very successful (sell) things. **m.** His wife refused (have) anything to do with it. **n.** I'm looking forward (see) you in London next weekend. **o.** He pleaded not guilty (rob) the bank. **p.** You should be ashamed (say) such a thing. **q.** His is an unusual method (teach) English. **r.** You start the machine (push) this button here. **s.** We don't have the money (go) to Australia. **t.** Have you ever tried your hand (write) a poem? **u.** That holiday will give me a chance (improve) my English. **v.** She had the strange idea (invite) all her enemies. **w.** I think I'd prefer (stay) with a family.

Transfer

1. Letter writing

You would like to take an English course in England during your next summer holiday(s). Write to St James's School, including the following points:

a. Received letter. Interested.
b. Your level (elementary – intermediate – advanced).
c. Special interests: Reading/Writing? Listening/Speaking? General/Commercial/Technical English? Meeting English people? Etc.
d. Intended length of stay, from . . . to . . . Full-day, half-day, part-time (4 hrs a week?) course?
e. Accommodation required.
f. Cost of course and accommodation?

```
                        February 10, 1983


Ms Hilary Franklin
St James's School of English
37 St James's Street
London SW1A 1HG
England


Dear Ms Franklin,

      XXXXXXXXXXXXXXXXXXXXXXXXXXXXXXXXXX
XXXXXXXXXXXXXXXXXXXXXXXXXXXXXXXXXXXXXX
XXXXXXXXXXXXXXXXXXXXXXX

      XXXXXXXXXXXXXXXXXXXXXXXXXXXXXXX
XXXXXXXXXXXXXXXXXXXXXXXXXXXXXXXXXXXXXXX
XXXXXXXXXXXXXXXXXXXXXXXXXXXXXXXXXXXXXXXXX
XXXXXXXX

      XXXXXXXXXXXXXXXXXXXXXXXXXXXXXX
XXXXXXXXXXXXXXXXXXXXXXXXXXXXXXXXXXXXXXXXX
XXXXXXXXXXXXXXXXXXXXXXXXXXXXXXXXXXXXXX
XXXXXXXXXXXXXXXXXXXXXXXXXXXX

                        Yours sincerely,
```

2. Pair work

a. A neighbour of yours (student A) had a few years of English at school but says (s)he has forgotten most of it. Student B tries to persuade A to brush up his/her English and suggests ways in which this could be done.

Arguments
Uses of English: travel, business, job, helping the kids with their homework, world events in the news, general education

Phrases
I think you ought to / should . . .
Wouldn't it be a good idea if you . . .
Why don't you . . .

b. Your partner, who is 45, says (s)he is too old to learn a foreign language. Try to convince him/her that this is not so.

9A

A

He's having his shoes polished

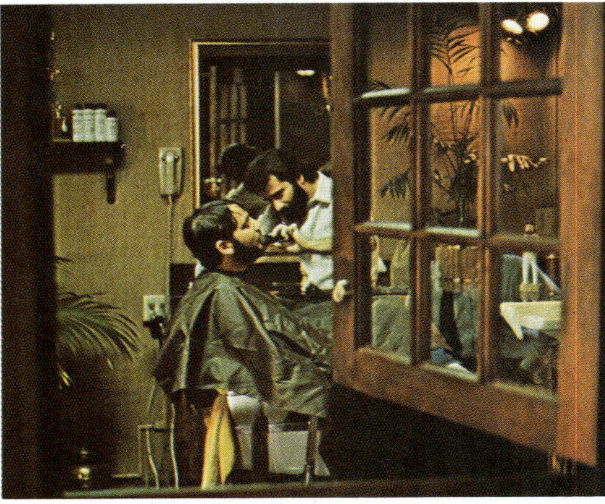

He's having his hair cut

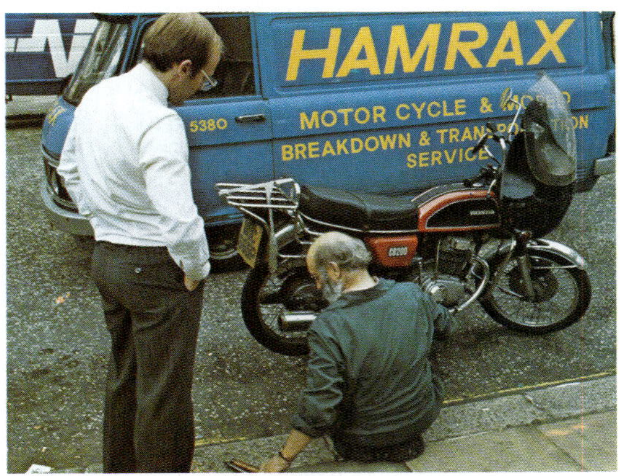

He's getting his motorcycle repaired

Warm-up

Getting things done

John and Susan want to get a number of things done before they go on holiday:
Susan's got a hole in a tooth, so she's going to the dentist to have it filled.
John's hair is too long, so he's going to have it cut.
There's something wrong with their car, so they're taking it to the garage to . . .
John's trousers are dirty, so he's going . . .
Since John and Susan will be staying at the same place for four weeks, they'll have their mail . . .

Now *you* talk about things you get done or don't (like to) get done, things you will/ won't have to get done, etc.

Wash the car?
Repair your TV / cassette recorder / . . .?
Redecorate the sitting room?
Paint the kitchen / garden fence?
Mend your shoes?
Let out your trousers?
Alter a dress?
Vaccinate the dog?
Develop a film?
Make prints of a film?
Test your eyes?
Renew your passport?
Take your photograph?

Examples:
I don't like to have my photograph taken.
We can't afford to have our car washed, we wash it ourselves.
I can't see very well, I think I must have my eyes tested.
I think I'll have to have my passport renewed.
Etc.

Texts

Old folk victims of teenage terror

ELDERLY people in Overhill Drive, Patcham, live in fear of youths who throw stones at them, smash windows and pull up bushes from gardens.

"I had six windows broken several months ago while I was away," says Mrs Dorothy Taylor. "A neighbour of ours had her wooden fence pulled down and washing stolen off the line."

78-year-old Mary Thomas dare not go out in the evening for fear of the youths, who sit in the street smoking and swearing or throwing stones up at the street lights. On one occasion not long ago, an elderly woman was hit by a stone and knocked unconscious, Mrs Thomas says.

In a letter to the Council the people living in the Overhill Drive area are protesting about "insufficient police protection".

A police spokesman said: "There are plenty of patrols but the problem is how to be in the right place at the right time. We have car, motorcycle and foot patrols, and it takes no time at all to get someone to a trouble spot.

"People should ring us as soon as they hear something, not the next day. All they have to do is pick up the phone and dial 999. It doesn't cost them anything."

2. Comprehension – Please complete

a. According to the newspaper article, the youngsters have . . .
b. One elderly woman was knocked unconscious by . . .
c. The people living in the Overhill Drive area think they're not sufficiently . . .
d. The police say they can't . . .
e. When there's trouble somewhere, people should . . .
f. If you make a 999 call, you . . .

3. Listening for the main facts

Before reading the text "The new playground", listen to the recording with the printed text covered. As you listen, try to find answers to the following questions:

a. Why are some of the speakers against the Council's plans for the new playground?
b. What could the Council do to make the playground acceptable to those living near it?
c. In what condition is the site of the planned playground at the moment?

The new playground

A So the playground's going to be built after all.
B Yes, it looks as if there's nothing we can do about it.
C I wouldn't mind a playground if it was on the other side of the field away from the bungalows.
A I'm not keen to have a playground right up to my fence either.
D It depends on how you look at it. The children deserve a place where they can play in safety, don't they?

9B/C

B No doubt about that. But not so near the houses. It's bad enough as it is. With the children playing football there we're getting balls kicked into our garden all the time.
C We've had tiles broken on the roof . . .
A . . . and we've had some greenhouse windows broken. I'd hate to have a playground right next to our garden.
D But there's nowhere they can put a playground where it isn't near someone. Besides, a real playground probably means less trouble than a piece of wasteland that's part playground, part rubbish dump. I think the Council's plans for developing the field are fair enough.
C Couldn't we have bushes and trees planted between the actual play area and the gardens?
D I think that's an excellent suggestion. If they put the playing equipment on the side of the field furthest away from the houses, there should be enough space for bushes and trees. Let's hope the Council is prepared to be generous.

C Insight and practice

1. Have something done (→ G21)

The structure *have something done* has two different meanings. Explain the difference in the following pairs of sentences.

He had two teeth filled. He had two teeth knocked out.
She had her car repaired. She had her car stolen.
She had her children vaccinated. She had her children taken from her.
We're having some new bushes planted. We're having bushes pulled up in our garden all the time.

2. (Prep. +) Pronoun + infinitive or -ing form (→ G19, G20)

Do you want (I/get) you something? Do you want me to get you something?
They insisted (I/come) with them. They insisted on my/me coming with them.

a. The principal advised (I/take) an intensive course.
b. Can you imagine (she/work) in a shop?
c. Did you manage (persuade/she/come) to the party?
d. There's no danger (they/go) broke.
e. Are you worried (she/drink) too much?
f. When a policeman sees a man swaying, it's reasonable (he/think) that he's drunk.
g. The police suspect (he/kill) the girl.

Transfer

1. Young man out of work

Supply suitable verb forms.

JIMMY ROBINSON (leave) school two years ago and (now be) out of work for six months.

"My days are just (spend) shopping for my mum, playing pool and watching TV," he says.

"I get £19 a week on the dole. I give half to my mother, and after (buy) cigarettes – what else is left?

"I've (do) everything (get) a job. The last job I (go) for was as a guard with British Rail. I (not get) it.

"I also (try) for jobs in shops, but it was the same story."

Questions on the text:

a. How old do you think Jimmy is?
b. What do you think Jimmy did after leaving school?
c. How do you think Jimmy feels about his situation?
d. What would you do if you were in Jimmy's position?

2. The teenagers' problems

The old people in 9B1 have a problem: they are "terrorized" by teenagers. But the youngsters probably have problems too. Talk about the young folk's problems. Why do they hang around the streets? Why are they aggressive?

3. Group discussion: The new pub

There is no pub on the new housing estate where you live. A brewery wants to build a pub on the estate. You, the residents, discuss the plan, some of you arguing in favour of the pub, others against it.

Possible pros and cons:
Good/Bad for social/family life.
People get to know each other / spend more money on drink.
Rooms for clubs, family parties, etc.
Noise (jukebox).
Bad example to children.
Etc.

Time for a break 3

I don't smoke.
I don't smoke.

How are you?
How are you?

Have a nice weekend.
Have a nice weekend.

Would you pass the sugar, please?
Would you pass the sugar, please?

I didn't manage to get a ticket.
I didn't manage to get a ticket.

bus.

Give my regards to Pat.
Give my regards to Pat.

Do you mind if I sit here?
Do you mind if I sit here?

Can I talk to Gary, please?
Can I talk to Gary, please?

Start

Finish

How did you come?
How did you come?

Would you like some tea?
Would you like some tea?

Will Philip be coming to the wedding?
Will Philip be coming to the wedding?

What about going for a swim?
What about going for a swim?

FIND TH

By ca
How awfu
I'd love to
I'm an enginee
It doesn't matte
No, I don't think so
No, not at al
Nor do
Not at al
Oh, bad luck
Oh, congratulations
Oh, I'm sorry to hear tha
Oh no, I can manage all right, thank you
Oh, that'd be nice. I'd love to

ANSWER

h, that's quite all right.
o do I.
hank you, I certainly will.
hanks, the same to you.
hat's all right.
ery well, thank you.
es, here you are.
es, hold on a moment.
es, I expect so.
es, it does, doesn't it?
es, it is, isn't it?
es, let's.
es, please.

I was wondering if you'd like to come to the cinema with me.
I was wondering if you'd like to come to the cinema with me.

I'm afraid I'm rather late.
I'm afraid I'm rather late.

I've passed my exam.
I've passed my exam.

Our dog's just died.
Our dog's just died.

Sorry to trouble you.
Sorry to trouble you.

It rained all the time we were in London.
It rained all the time we were in London.

Let me help you with your bags.
Let me help you with your bags.

Looks a bit like rain, doesn't it?
Looks a bit like rain, doesn't it?

What do you do?
What do you do?

What a lovely day!
What a lovely day!

Shall we go for a walk?
Shall we go for a walk?

Sorry to have kept you waiting.
Sorry to have kept you waiting.

Thank you for all the trouble you've taken.
Thank you for all the trouble you've taken.

10A/B

A Warm-up

Talking about the future: the year 2000 and after

Pair work: One student asks, another answers.
Will things be very different from the way they are today?

a. The "man in the street" – better or worse off?
b. Life in the big cities – more or less pleasant?
c. Cars on the roads – more or fewer? Differences from today's cars?
d. People still learning the same way as today? Bigger or smaller schools? Learning at home (computer, television)?
e. New methods of learning foreign languages?
f. Computers in every home? Uses?
g. Holidays on the moon?
h. Nuclear weapons banned, nuclear stockpiles destroyed, nuclear war avoided?
i. U.S. still most powerful country? Other superpowers?
j. People healthier, happier, freer, more religious than today?
k. People live longer, pay higher taxes, have more spare time, watch more TV?
l. More, or less, pollution, crime, terrorism, hunger, poverty, unemployment, democracy, freedom?

B Texts

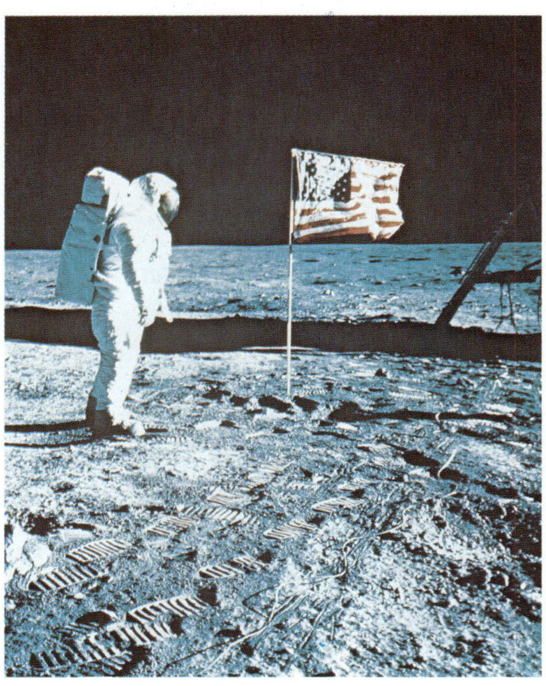

1. Predicting what lies ahead

In 1889, when the first petrol-driven cars were already on the roads, a British journal made the following prediction: "The ordinary 'horseless carriage' is at present a luxury for the wealthy; and although its price will probably fall in the future, it will never, of course, come into as common use as the bicycle."
And in 1948, 21 years before the first man set foot on the moon, a U.S. scientific journal wrote: "Landing on and moving around the moon offers so many serious problems for human beings that it may take science another 200 years to solve them."
"The future you shall know when it has come; before then, forget it," said a Greek poet about 24 centuries ago, but in spite of this advice predictions of the future have always found ready ears.
In 1888, an American journalist named

Croly published a book under the title *Glimpses of the Future*. This book, which the author intended "to be read now and judged in the year 2000", predicted among other things that India would become independent before 1950, that Russia would become the most powerful country beside the United States, that the business world would be controlled by a few big companies, that there would be motion pictures and aeroplanes, and that steam energy would be replaced by electricity and other power sources.

There are, indeed, some striking cases of predictions come true, but there are countless others which couldn't have been further from the truth, like the prediction, repeated again and again, that the world would end at a particular time.

Since the 1960s "futurology" has been established as a science which tries to forecast future developments mainly from present trends in society. To guess intelligently what the future may bring, futurologists use experts' forecasts, statistics and computers. Whether their methods produce better results than the good old crystal ball, only the future will show.

2. Comprehension and comment

a. What did the British journal predict about cars? Do you think it was a stupid prediction?
b. When did the first man set foot on the moon? – Putting a couple of men on the moon cost the U.S. taxpayer something like 25 billion dollars. Do you think that money should have been spent on something else?
c. The Bible says: "Do not worry about tomorrow; tomorrow will look after itself. Each day has troubles enough of its own." Compare this advice with that given by the Greek poet.
d. What do you think of the predictions made by Croly in 1888? What do you think enabled Croly to forecast future developments so successfully?
e. It has been predicted that the world will end around the year 2000. What do you think of such predictions?
f. What do you think of futurology as a science?

"Take the lift to the sixth floor, Mr Frensham. The computer will meet you there."

3. Glimpses of the future?

1986
A computer program beats the world chess champion.

1988
Most assembly-line workers have been replaced by robots.

1989
A computer makes an original scientific discovery and its program is considered worthy of a Nobel Prize.

By 1990
With petrol costs perhaps 10 times those of 1980, people own fewer cars, drive them less, and increasingly use streetcars, buses, taxis, car pools, motorcycles, mopeds, bicycles, etc., and their own two feet.
At least one country is blackmailed by terrorists who have a nuclear device.

1990
People have portable telephones. The telephone book is a minicomputer.

1992
The first human is brought back to life after being frozen and thawed.
27% of Americans are unable to read and write (1% in 1980).

By 2000
Electric vehicles come into widespread use.
If caught in the early stages, every kind of cancer can be cured.

By 2030
Everyone not living in the tropics is painfully aware that we are moving into another ice age.
A new source of power is found and used instead of oil, gas, and electricity.

Which of the predictions do you think are likely to come true, which not? (Reasons?) Which would be good news if they came true, which bad? (Reasons?)

If the year for which a prediction has been made is past, did it come true? If not, when do you think it might come true?

C Insight and practice

"Rail travel at high speed is not possible because passengers would be unable to breathe." (Prof. D. Lardner, 1793–1859)

"No large steamship will ever be able to cross the Atlantic, since it would require more coal than it can carry." (Prof. D. Lardner)

"You won't get very far in life." (A Munich schoolmaster to Albert Einstein, aged 10)

"We don't like their sound. Groups of guitars are on the way out." (Decca Recording Company when turning down the Beatles in 1962)

1. Indirect speech

Complete the following sentences, using indirect speech.
Professor Lardner thought that . . .
The professor also predicted . . .
When Albert Einstein was ten years old, his teacher told him . . .
The Decca people turned the Beatles down, saying . . .
In 1889, a British journal predicted that . . .
And in 1948, a U.S. scientific journal wrote that . . .

2. Conditional sentences: Complete the following sentences, expressing your own opinion (→ G11)

a. If most assembly-line workers were replaced by robots . . .
b. If petrol cost 10 times as much as it does now . . .
c. If terrorists got hold of a nuclear device . . .
d. If cancer could be cured . . .
e. If there was another ice age . . .
f. If everybody carried a telephone in their bag or pocket . . .
g. If all nuclear stockpiles were destroyed . . .
h. If the Decca Company hadn't turned the Beatles down . . .

D

Transfer

Orwell's 1984

"If you want a picture of the future, imagine a boot stamping on a human face – for ever."

This is the way one of the characters in George Orwell's novel *1984* sees the future. *1984* was published in 1949, shortly before Orwell's death in 1950.

The state of 1984 is a totalitarian police state ruled by an all-powerful "Big Brother". Public and private life are completely controlled by the Party. There is a two-way television set in every room so people can be watched all the time ("Big Brother is watching you").

a. What do you think made Orwell paint such a pessimistic picture of the future?
b. Do you think we are now nearer to the state described by Orwell than in 1949?
c. Are there any countries in the world now with a political system similar to that described by Orwell?
d. A boot stamping on a human face – do you think that is really a picture of man's future?
e. Try to explain how a two-way television set might work.
f. Talk about the scene from the film *1984* shown in the picture above.

11A

A Warm-up

Grand Puzzle

1	2	3	4		■	5	6	■	7		8	
9				■	10			■	11			
■		■	12	13								
14			■		■	15		■		■		■
16		■	17		18	■		■	19			20
	■	21				22	■	23		■	24	
	■		■	25						■	■	
26	27		■		■		■	28				
29			30						■	■	■	
31		■		■	32					33		
34						■	35					

ACROSS

1 Tobacco is to pipe as whisky is to . . . . .
5 Short for a city on California's coast
7 You can't wash properly without it
9 A gallon is much . . . . . than a litre
10 Trades Union Congress
11 Penny is to pound as . . . . . is to dollar
12 . . . . . calculators are light, fast and cheap
14 The place to go if you want a drink
15 The end of a boxing match
16 "The Singing Fool" whom many called "the world's greatest entertainer"
17 There was a time long, long . . . . . when people still had time
19 I wouldn't have thought . . . . . could happen
21 ". . . . . at the beginning and go on till you come to the end: then stop" *(Alice in Wonderland)*
23 An American soldier
24 Lufthansa
25 Fortunately they both had . . . . . for the night of the murder
26 Short for President Lincoln's first name
28 A country and the stuff fine teacups are made of
29 If two things are not alike, they're . . . . .
31 "To be, ... not to be – that is the question" *(Hamlet)*
32 Another word for "border"
34 If you send it by airmail, it'll arrive . . . . .
35 I haven't got it in cash, can I give you a . . . . .?

DOWN

1 General Motors
2 He reads two newspapers every day: the . . . . . paper and a national one
3 Short for "arrive"
4 Hear is to listen as . . . . . is to look
5 You need it at the slot machines
6 President Reagan was one
7 Welsh is to Wales as . . . . . is to Scotland
8 Rose is to flower as dog is to . . . . .
13 Another word for "baggage"
14 An island in the West Indies
17 Atomic energy or American English
18 We'll run out of it sooner or later
20 Shakespeare wrote for it
21 The meat of a cow
22 A river and a republic in West Africa
27 "Ball pen" is another word for it
30 Most people like it better than work
33 If you have one of 150, you're a genius

Text

1. A letter from David

Dear Mark,

I'm typing this lying on the couch with my right leg in plaster. I was dashing downstairs to catch the postman yesterday morning when I missed a step, slipped and fell down the stairs. I was lucky not to break my neck. At the hospital they diagnosed a broken ankle and nasty bruises all over my body. I could have kicked myself - but I can't now!

Incidentally, the machine I'm typing this letter on is an electronic miracle. When I first saw it, I thought it was just a toy. It's hardly bigger than a packet of typing paper and weighs about five pounds, or - to use the built-in calculator - 5×0.4536= 2.268 kilograms! Far from being a toy, this little machine has an electronic memory, i.e. there's a display that shows you what you're typing so you can correct any mistakes before the text is actually printed out. There are one-third more letters and symbols than on a normal machine, e.g. square brackets [ ] and the symbols for pounds (£), dollars ($) and cents (¢). The tiny thing runs off four batteries and is practically silent. - Amazing, isn't it?

"Big impresses, but small sells" - that seems to be one of the important discoveries of our time. After mini calculators, mini cassette recorders, mini typewriters and wristwatch television - you wonder what will come next.

2. Comprehension and extension

a. Why does David have his leg in plaster?
b. Why does David say he could have kicked himself?
c. Describe the typewriter David is using.
d. What's one pound in grams or kilograms?
e. Look at the letter typed by David. Does the print look like normal typewriter print?
f. "Big impresses, but small sells." Give examples to show what this means.
g. Apart from mini calculators, mini cassette recorders, mini typewriters, and wristwatch TV, what other "mini" things do you use at home or at work? Try to describe them.

C Insight and practice

1. Some – any (→ G8)

a. We got **something** to eat on the plane.
b. We didn't get **anything** to eat.
c. Did you get **anything** to eat?

Remember:
Some is used in positive statements (a).
Any is used in negative statements (b) and in ("real"/"open") questions (c).

Put in some, somebody/someone, something, somewhere or any, anybody/anyone, anything, anywhere

a. Is there . . . . . I can do for you? – Yes, there's . . . . . you could do. I haven't got . . . . . cigarettes left – could you go out and get . . . . .?
b. We hardly ever get . . . . . sunshine these days. Can't we go . . . . . where it's nice and warm? Why don't we get . . . . . . brochures from the travel agent so we can start planning our next holiday – that'll give us . . . . . to look forward to.
c. I need . . . . . to help me move the furniture.
d. Can you imagine . . . . . buying sunglasses for £1,100? – Yes, I know . . . . . who might be crazy enough to do just that.
e. It's a pity there aren't . . . . . trees in the front garden. Couldn't we at least have . . . . . bushes planted there?
f. It seems nobody has time for . . . . . these days.
g. I've got . . . . . problems I can't talk to . . . . . about.
h. I wouldn't lose . . . . . sleep over . . . . . as unimportant as that.
i. There was no one to be seen . . . . .

2. Relative clauses

I use a typewriter at the office.
It's an electronic miracle.
The typewriter I use at the office is an electronic miracle.

The taxi he . . . was red

Make two sentences into one

a. I've bought a chess computer. It's said to have beaten two grandmasters.
b. They're going to build a playground. It'll be very close to the bungalows.
c. She took some photos of him. They're quite interesting.
d. We've got our car in a car park. It closes at 7 p.m.
e. We had lunch at a hotel. It was very elegant.
f. I talked to a policeman. He wasn't very helpful.
g. David Croly made some predictions in 1888. Some of them have actually come true.
h. He was taken to a hospital. It doesn't seem to be very good.

Transfer

1. Pair work: React to what your partner says

A	"Do they accept cheques at the casino?"
B	"I'm sure they do." / "I don't know." / "Yes, why shouldn't they?" *Etc.*
A	"It's rather cold in here."
B	"Yes, it is, isn't it? "/ "Oh – do you think so? I'm feeling rather warm." *Etc.*

a. "Do you think it'll rain tomorrow?"
b. "Did you know that Ronald Reagan was a film actor before he went into politics?"
c. "Have you any idea what President Lincoln's Christian name was?"
d. "I wonder how many litres there are in a gallon."
e. "Let's go for a drink when this is over, shall we?"
f. "The price of cigarettes has gone up again."
g. "I've lost my ball pen."
h. "I fell down the stairs yesterday and almost broke my neck."
i. "I won $200 at the slot machines last night."
j. "My son's got an IQ of 150."
k. "The Queen was sitting next to me at the theatre last night."
l. "The police actually asked me if I had an alibi for last Wednesday night."

2. Group discussion: Wristwatch television

The wristwatch TV set: just a toy or useful to have?
Size? Weight? Features? Uses? Price?

3. Letter writing

You are Mark, who got the letter from David in 11B1. Write an answer, including the following points:
a. David's accident.
b. Express interest in David's typewriter: Make? Price?
c. Comment on the slogan "Big impresses, but small sells".
d. Wish David a speedy recovery ("I hope you get better soon").

4. Role play: Selling a Walkman

Student A is a sales assistant trying to sell a Walkman to student B, a customer.

12A/B

A

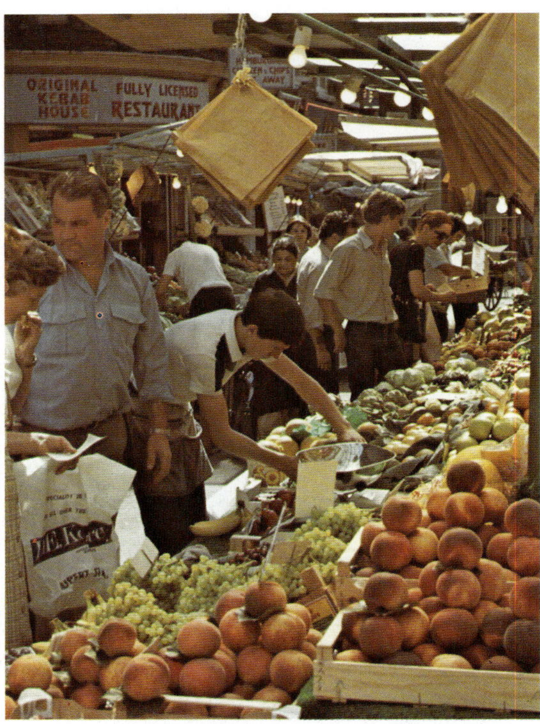

Warm-up

Pair work: Eating and drinking habits

Students ask and answer questions about their eating and drinking habits.

a. Ask your partner what (s)he usually eats/ drinks for breakfast/supper.
b. Does (s)he eat a lot of meat / fish / bread / eggs / tinned food / . . .?
c. . . . sometimes eat oysters / chew tobacco / bake . . . own bread?
d. . . . a health-food fan / vegetarian / big eater?
e. . . . eat as much as (s)he likes or try to stay slim?
f. . . . count calories?
g. . . . drink coffee/alcohol?

Fresh fruit at the market – is it "unsprayed"?

B Texts

1. [cassette symbol]

The trend in food

THE TASTE of Britain's consumers is changing and supermarkets all over the country are having to change as well to keep up with demand.

Everything that's fresh, pure, and natural is in. Convenience foods are giving way to health foods. Fruit juices, wet fish and natural jams and marmalades are the order of the day, and so are bran, wholemeal, and brown rice.

Bread is increasingly being eaten for enjoyment, not just as a filler. There's a trend towards brown and wholemeal bread, and people want it fresh.

More and more families are switching to free-range eggs because they're fresher, taste better and look more appetizing than battery-produced ones.

Chicken top of Britain's menu

CHICKEN has replaced roast beef as the most popular Sunday meal for most British families.

The British are now eating more chicken than beef, pork, and lamb. About 400 million birds are consumed each year.

The boom in chicken, either as whole birds or in portions, is due to its price advantage over other meat, which is made possible by intensive battery production.

2. Comprehension

Changing eating habits

People used to eat a lot of . . . but now . . .
. . . is/are giving way to . . .
. . . is/are becoming very popular and so is/are . . .
There's a trend towards . . .
Bread used to be . . . but now . . .
Brown bread is becoming . . .
Free-range eggs are . . . because . . .
Roast beef is being . . .

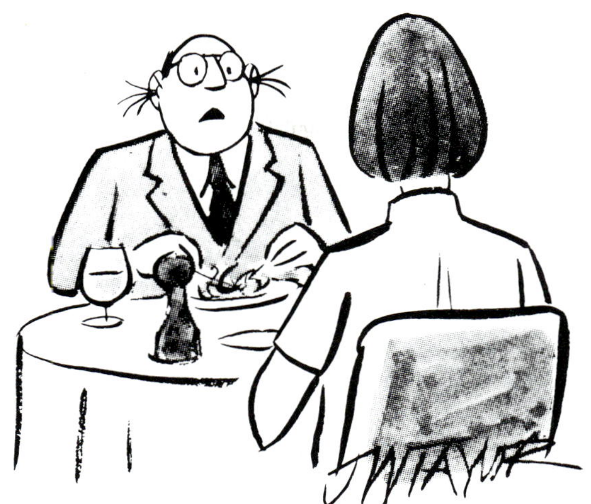

"I read an article this morning that says you can have too much fibre."

3. Eating and drinking habits of some famous people

The Frenchman Balzac was not only one of the greatest writers of all time but also an extraordinary eater. At one meal he ate a dozen cutlets, a duck, two partridges, and 110 oysters, not to mention various desserts.

The British poet Lord Byron tried to stay slim by living on biscuits and soda water for days and chewing tobacco to keep his mind off his hunger.

Tennis champion Billie Jean King counts calories to avoid overeating. She stays away from red meat, which can have twice the calories of fish. If she has a potato, she'll just add a little butter. She avoids food with white flour and white sugar, and instead chooses wholemeal bread or bran muffins.

George Bernard Shaw took light and frugal meals and avoided meat, tea, and alcohol. A tall man, he never weighed more than 9 stone and lived to the age of 94.

Even in his old age the French philosopher Voltaire is said to have drunk 50 cups of coffee daily. When someone remarked to him that coffee was a slow poison, he replied: "I think it must be, for I've been drinking it for 65 years and am not dead yet." He died at the age of 83.

4. Comprehension and extension: Conditional sentences (→ G11)

Try to complete the following sentences.

a. If Balzac had eaten less, . . .
b. If Lord Byron hadn't chewed tobacco, . . .
c. If Shaw hadn't eaten so frugally, . . .
d. If Billie Jean King didn't count calories, . . .
e. If she ate more red meat, . . .

12 C/D

C Insight and practice

1. Put in adverbs ending in -ly

a. Bread is . . . . . being eaten for enjoyment.
b. Animals are often treated . . . . . before being slaughtered.
c. The taste of Britain's consumers is . . . . . changing.
d. He . . . . . ever drinks alcohol.
e. The salad is . . . . . made.
f. She . . . . . counts the calories of everything she eats.
g. He looked . . . . . at the biscuits but didn't dare to take one.
h. The dessert tasted . . . . . good.
i. You can't . . . . . live on 1,500 calories a day if you have to work.
j. You'd . . . . . lose weight if you ate less.

2. Pair work: So/Nor . . . I (→ G18)

One student makes a statement; his/her partner says that the statement applies to him/her too.

I often watch TV in the evening. So do I.
I'm not a vegetarian. Nor am I.

a. I'm trying to stay slim.
b. I've never weighed more than 9 stone.
c. I never count calories.
d. I like wholemeal bread.
e. I couldn't eat a dozen cutlets.
f. I won't be going away this summer.
g. I can't sing very well.

D Transfer

Never mind the calories – ice cream is fun!

1. Silly questions?

a. Why do some people count the calories of what they eat?
b. What's the advantage of convenience food?
c. Why is wholemeal bread regarded as healthier than white bread?
d. Why do people drink coffee?
e. What's the difference between battery-produced and free-range eggs?

2. Folk wisdom?

Say in your own words what the following proverbs mean, giving examples, if possible. Do you agree with the opinions expressed in the proverbs?

An apple a day keeps the doctor away.

In wine there is truth.

Hunger is the best sauce.

One man's meat is another man's poison.

3. Group discussion: Vegetarianism – pros and cons

Discuss the following arguments, possibly adding some of your own.

Pros	Cons
It's wrong to rear animals – often inhumanely (battery production!) – only to kill them for food. Animals are often slaughtered in a cruel way. They also suffer on the way to the slaughterhouse. If everyone had to slaughter his own meat, most people would be vegetarians. Eating meat makes people restless, aggressive, and cruel. On average, meat eaters drink more alcohol than vegetarians. Animal fats aren't good for your health. Animals are now so stuffed with chemicals it's hard to know what you're eating. Vegetarians live longer than meat eaters.	If all people became vegetarians, that would not prevent the killing of animals. E.g., if cows are to be kept for milk and cheese, then bulls would have to be destroyed as non-productive. Whether one is a vegetarian or not has no influence on one's character. After all, Hitler was a vegetarian! Vegetarian food is often not very appetizing. If it is, it's expensive. Vegetarians who eat eggs, milk, and cheese are not true vegetarians, for they can only get those things if other people eat meat. Most vegetarians (in Europe at any rate) are white-collar workers. If they had to do heavy work, they would have to give up being vegetarians.

4. Animals and us

a. The British philosopher Jeremy Bentham once remarked about animals: "The question is not, Can they *think*? nor Can they *talk*? but, Can they *suffer*?" – How would you answer Bentham's question?
b. If your answer to (a) is yes, how do you feel about the way billions of egg-laying hens are kept all their lives nowadays – in batteries of tiny cages which make it impossible for them to move?
c. How could consumers force egg producers to give up battery production?
d. Do you think it would be possible for all the people of the world to become vegetarians? If not, what could people do to at least reduce the suffering of animals?
e. An English churchman once said: "We have treated animals so badly that beyond doubt, if they were able to develop a religion, they would picture the Devil in human form." What do *you* think?

Time for a break 4

START

1 He gives twice …

2 A person … makes nothing.

3 People … should not throw stones.

4 He laughs best …

5 The man … is a fool.

6 God helps those …

7 Every country has the government …

8 He travels the fastest …

9 A thing … is dear at any price.

10 The people … were extremely friendly.

11 People … are not true vegetarians.

12 The photos … are really very good.

13 The hotel … was very pleasant.

14 All's well …

15 It's the unexpected …

16 Most of the book became best sell

17 Never make threats …

18 who makes no mistakes

19 we stayed with c our last holiday

20 that ends well

The Relative Clause Game

FINISH

21 who live in glass houses

22 you can't carry out

23 you don't want

24 who eat eggs

25 we stayed at last summer

26 who travels alone

27 it deserves

28 who help themselves

29 he wrote

30 you took of us

31 who laughs last

32 that always happens

33 who told you that

34 who gives quickly

13 A/B

A Warm-up

The Jumbled-Word Game

Put the letters in the right order to form the name of a famous personality.
The circled letters express a truth relevant to the topic of this Unit.

1. REGJAG
2. MANRUT
3. EARNAG
4. CYBROS
5. DYNEKEN
6. HIPCLAN
7. SLEARCH
8. NELOR

a. Say a sentence or two about each personality.
b. What's the "two-word truth"?

B Texts

1.

Handguns banned in San Francisco

IN 1982 San Francisco became the first major American city to pass a law forbidding people to own handguns.

"This law will help us make our streets and homes safe for everyone," said Mayor Dianne Feinstein.

Mrs Feinstein became mayor in 1978 when her predecessor and a supervisor were shot in City Hall by another supervisor. Those killings started a local drive for stronger gun control.

There were 126 murders in San Francisco in 1981, with handguns involved in half of them. Guns were also commonly used in robberies, rapes, and other violent crimes, including attacks on tourists.

Under the new law, the illegal possession of handguns may be punished by up to 30 days in jail and a $500 fine.

The National Rifle Association, which strongly defends the right of Americans to own firearms, protested against the new law, saying: "It will make criminals out of thousands of law-abiding citizens."

2.

Georgia city outlaws non-possession of guns

IN 1982, the small town of Kennesaw, Georgia, became the first community in the United States – and probably the world – where every family was required by law to own a gun and keep it loaded and in good working order.

Darvin Purdy, Kennesaw's 38-year-old mayor, said he had received hundreds of letters supporting the city council's decision. "Amen to the only perfect solution to the high crime rate," wrote a man from California.

The new gun law put Kennesaw on the map and made its mayor a popular personality on radio and TV talk shows, where he declared: "I'd like to see high schools introduce gun-handling courses."

While the police reported a sharp drop in burglaries (from 55 in 1981), Kennesaw's Main Street gun store was doing a brisk trade – not only in guns but also in signs reading: "Never Mind the Dog – Beware of the Owner".

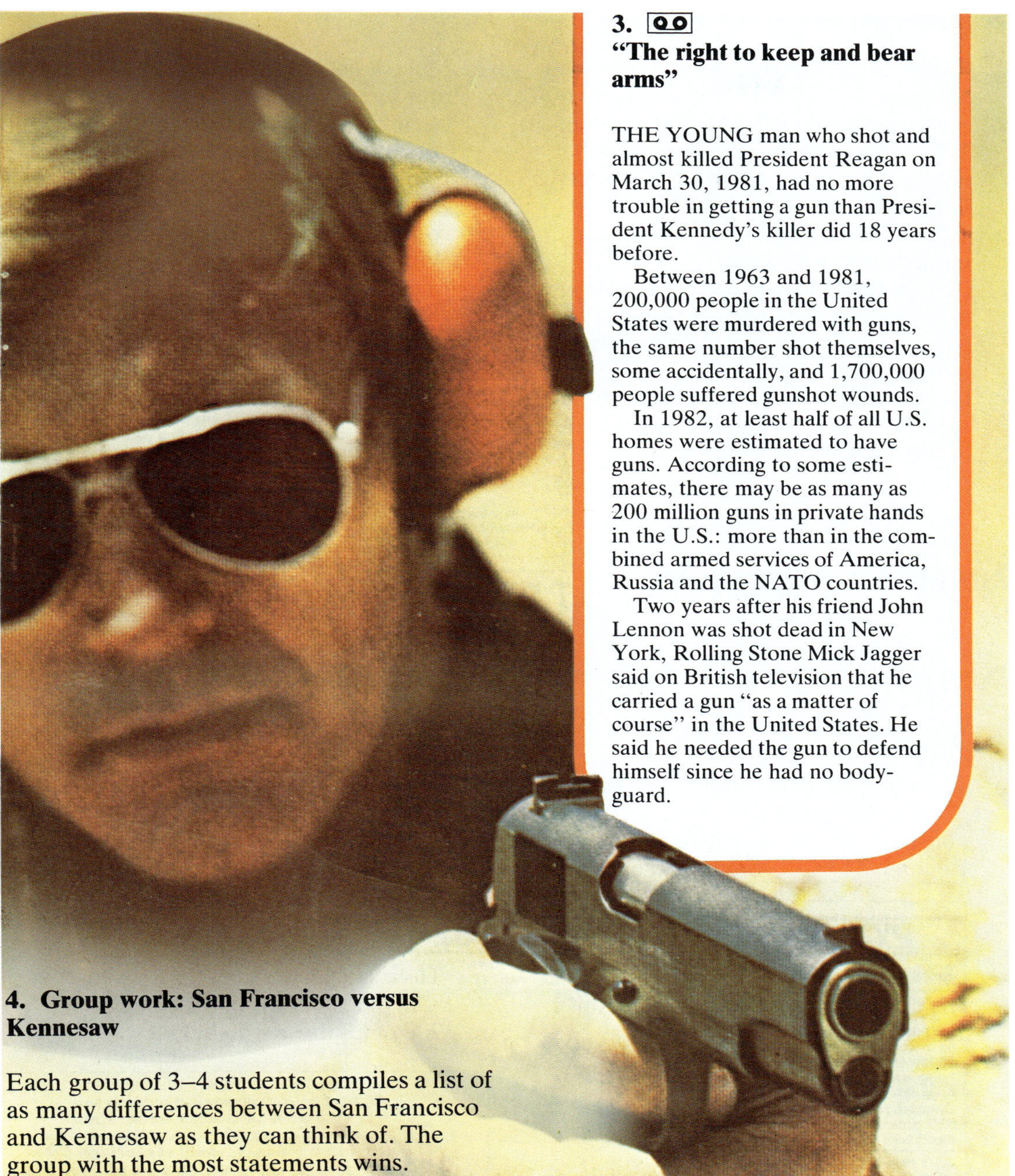

3. "The right to keep and bear arms"

THE YOUNG man who shot and almost killed President Reagan on March 30, 1981, had no more trouble in getting a gun than President Kennedy's killer did 18 years before.

Between 1963 and 1981, 200,000 people in the United States were murdered with guns, the same number shot themselves, some accidentally, and 1,700,000 people suffered gunshot wounds.

In 1982, at least half of all U.S. homes were estimated to have guns. According to some estimates, there may be as many as 200 million guns in private hands in the U.S.: more than in the combined armed services of America, Russia and the NATO countries.

Two years after his friend John Lennon was shot dead in New York, Rolling Stone Mick Jagger said on British television that he carried a gun "as a matter of course" in the United States. He said he needed the gun to defend himself since he had no bodyguard.

4. Group work: San Francisco versus Kennesaw

Each group of 3–4 students compiles a list of as many differences between San Francisco and Kennesaw as they can think of. The group with the most statements wins.

»...the right of the people to keep and bear arms shall not be infringed.«
(From the Second Amendment to the U.S. Constitution, 1791)

13B/C

5. Comprehension and comment

a. 57,000 Americans lost their lives in the Vietnam War (1961–75); nearly 30,000 Americans were killed in car accidents in 1979. Compare these figures with the number of people killed with guns in the U.S.
b. Why do many Americans consider it important to own a gun?
c. Do you think Mayor Feinstein was right in saying that San Francisco's gun-control law would make streets and homes safer? Why (not)?
d. Do you think the sharp drop in burglaries reported by Kennesaw's police was due to the new gun law? (Reasons?)
e. Make a list of prominent Americans murdered with guns. Would they have been killed if it had been more difficult to get guns?
f. Explain the reaction of the National Rifle Association to San Francisco's gun-control law. What are they really saying? What's your opinion?

Say in your own words what this sign means

C Insight and practice

Put in -self/-selves pronouns where necessary

a. You might have killed . . . . . playing with that gun.
b. If you don't stop that noise, I'll complain . . . . . to your teacher.
c. Consumers' tastes are changing . . . . . all the time.
d. It's still not clear whether they were shot or whether they shot . . . . .
e. He didn't introduce . . . . ., so I don't know his name.
f. The chicken cages are so small that it's impossible for the hens to move . . . . .
g. What can a woman do to defend . . . . . against an attacker?
h. I could have kicked . . . . . when I noticed that I'd lost my wallet.
i. Get . . . . . something to drink, folks!
j. Be careful with these papers – we can't afford . . . . . to lose them.
k. I think we can congratulate . . . . . on a job well done.
l. The economic situation has not improved . . . . .
m. People who say something like that should be ashamed of . . . . .
n. Whether we like it or not, history does repeat . . . . .
o. The robbers threatened her with a gun, but she refused . . . . . to hand over the money.
p. "Do not worry . . . . . about tomorrow; tomorrow will look after . . . . ."
q. "How are you feeling . . . . . today?" – "Oh, much better, thanks."
r. God helps those who help . . . . .

We should look long and carefully at ourselves before we pass judgment on others. (Molière, 1622–1673)

Transfer

1. Pair work: React to what your partner says

a. "People in this country should be allowed to own handguns."
b. "I don't know how the police manage in Britain – they don't carry guns, you know!"
c. "If you go out at night in New York or Atlanta, it's always safer to have a loaded gun in your pocket."
d. "There would be fewer burglaries in this country if every householder had a gun."
e. "There should be courses in self-defence at adult-education centres."
f. "If everybody was taught first aid at school, there would be less violence."
g. "If it weren't for the U.S. Constitution's Second Amendment, John F. Kennedy and John Lennon would still be alive today."
h. "Bring back the birch and the death penalty. Then there'll be less crime in our society."
i. "If there was less violence on TV, people would be more peaceful."

"Of course their intelligence is carefully bred out of them . . ."

2. Class discussion: Guns or first aid?

Some Americans would like to see gun-handling courses introduced at high schools; others think that first aid should be taught to all students in primary and secondary education.
The class discusses the pros and cons of both suggestions and then has a vote:
For/Against gun-handling courses?
For/Against first-aid courses?

A first-aid class

14A

A Warm-up

Pair work: Talking about yourself

Talk about things that you would write about in a letter to relatives or friends:
Things you did or that happened recently.
What you've been doing lately.
Problems you have.
How/What friends or members of your family are doing. *Etc.*
The partner reacts by asking for more details, making comments, asking how long something has been going on, etc.

A Rita has started her apprenticeship.
B Oh, has she? How does she like it?

A Oliver has just finished school.
B Oh, has he? He must be glad it's all over. What's he going to do?

A Danny spends most of his spare time playing around with his computer.
B All the kids do these days, don't they? How long has he had one?
Etc.

Texts

1. Back from a vacation

September 9, 1983

Dear Susanne, Klaus, and Daniela,

Now that we've returned from our exciting trip, we can look back with many happy memories. One of the most wonderful things about it was the time we spent with you. We will long remember that lovely evening in ...

I'm enclosing some pictures we took of you. I wish we could have taken one of all of us together.

I'm also enclosing a clipping which you might enjoy reading - to prepare you for your trip to the United States.

My husband's brother, who is a doctor, was in an automobile accident while we were gone. He's in the hospital in serious condition. The girl who hit him was driving down the wrong side of the street during a rainstorm.

We're very fond of you three and feel as if we've known you forever. We do hope that you'll be able to come to our country and visit us. We've got plenty of room for you to stay with us.

We send our love to your mother and father and to each of you.

Fondly, Ann

2. Comprehension

a. Why did Ann write the above letter? What happened before it?
b. From the letter, how long do you think Ann has known Susanne, Klaus and Daniela?
c. What might "the clipping" be about?
d. The man who had the accident: was he in a car when it happened?

3. Letter writing

Answer Ann's letter as if you were Susanne or Klaus.

a. Thanks for letter. Comment on photos, clipping.
b. Your memories. Your photos (enclosed).
c. Wishes for speedy recovery.
d. Trip to U.S. possible?
e. Your feelings of friendship.

Air Mail
Mrs. Ann Phillips
52 Green Bay Road
Wilmette, Ill. 60091
U.S.A.

4. Letter from Illinois

Dear ...

Sorry I haven't written but we've had some problems lately. James has been having trouble at work, I've been laid off (after 16 years with the same company, can you imagine the shock?), and Andy has been in bad shape too (growing pains? too much stress at school?). Now James has an ulcer and my blood pressure is high. Not surprising, is it?

Two weeks ago today our cat, Bella, died. We were all very sad. She was so beautiful and well-mannered and - yes! - intelligent. She watched TV if it was her kind of program. She liked cartoon movies but lost interest when news or sports came on. She absolutely hated "Dallas"! She was a lazy cat but extremely sensitive. The moment we mentioned the vet, she'd be out the window. She was 15. We miss her very much.

But there's some good news too. Aunt Marjorie, who was 89 last July, passed her driver's test with flying colors - and just yesterday got home from the hospital, where she had all sorts of tests. The doctor said nothing was wrong - all the tests came out perfect. Isn't that something! She sends you her love.

It's snowing today and everything looks so beautiful. We're going out to buy our Christmas tree tomorrow, so we can decorate it Sunday.

Forgive me for not writing earlier. We do appreciate your friendship and sincerely hope you're all well - and that you'll have a wonderful, blessed Christmas. This snow we're having here certainly puts us into the mood for Christmas - our garden looks like a fairyland.

Love to all of you, Betty

A Christmas card

5. Comprehension and extension

a. What kind of trouble may James have been having at work?
b. Does Betty go out to work?
c. "Andy has been in bad shape" – what does that mean?
d. What may be the cause of James's ulcer?
e. Can you believe all the things Betty says about Bella, the cat?
f. Did Aunt Marjorie learn to drive at 89?
g. Why did Aunt Marjorie go to hospital?
h. About what time of the year do you think the letter was written? (Reasons?)
i. Is the letter likely to have been written to a relative? Why (not)?

6. American English

Look at the two letters again. Can you spot any expressions or spellings in them which are American rather than British English?

7. Letter writing

Answer Betty's letter, reacting to what she wrote and telling her about some recent happenings in your life.

Insight and practice

C

Present perfect, present, or past? (→ G10)

Please complete.

a. I (know) her since she was a child.
b. She's never been an easy person to work with but I (like) her.
c. Uncle Dick (have) an accident some time ago and (be) still in hospital.
d. We (have) trouble with the car ever since we bought it.
e. "How long (you have) your computer?" – "I got it last Christmas."
f. The police in Britain (not carry) guns.
g. Nearly 60,000 Americans (lose) their lives in the Vietnam War.
h. It (snow) for 36 hours. If it (not stop) soon,we'll be snowed in completely.
i. The reporter asked him if he (own) a gun.
j. Let's look for a place to have lunch. I (have) no breakfast this morning.
k. I (not be) too well lately.
l. I (wish) you were here.

Transfer

D

Letter writing

You've just got back from a holiday on the English south coast, where you met and became friends with a nice English couple. Write them a letter, mentioning – among other things – the nasty surprise you got on entering your house/flat.

burglars
terrible mess
turn out the drawers
break things
steal . . .

15A

A Warm-up

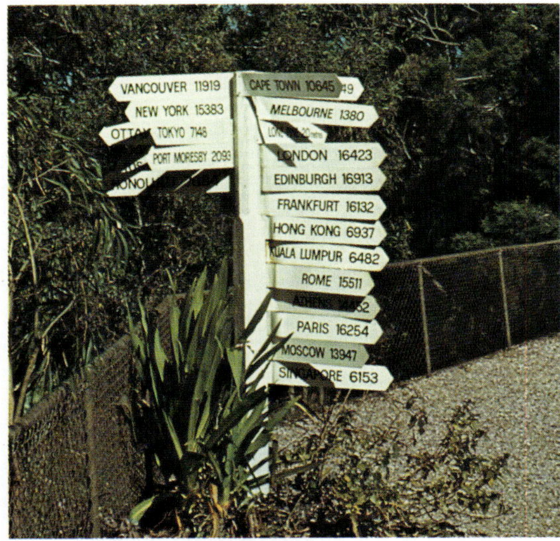

Read the distances aloud.
Where might this signpost be? (Reasons?)
Do you suppose the distances given are in miles or kilometres?

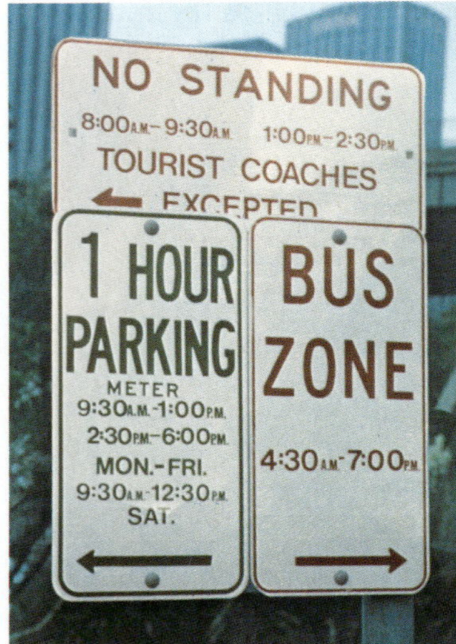

Confusing, isn't it? Are cars allowed to wait here at five in the afternoon? Where and how long can you park at 12.30 p.m. on weekdays?

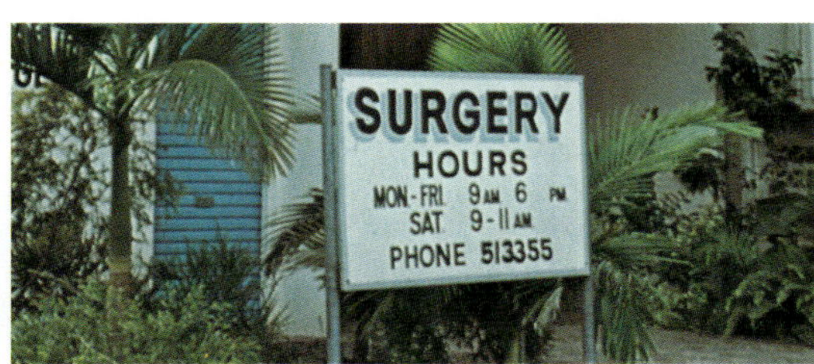

Who works in this house?
What kind of people come here?

What kind of place is this?
In what country? (Reasons?)
What is the woman doing?

Where do you think this sign is?
Say in your own words what it means.

Texts

1. [cassette icon]

Dismissed for swearing at the boss

WAREHOUSEMAN Geoffrey Gray had been working for six hours, unloading 19 tons of carpeting.

He was tired and fed up, and when his boss, transport manager Patrick Dixon, came in demanding to know about an order for 20 tins of floor polish, he lost his temper and told him to "bugger off".

Even though Mr Gray had worked for the company for two years with no previous complaints against him, managing director David Johnson decided that dismissal was the only answer.

Geoffrey Gray thought this was unfair and applied to an industrial tribunal.

a. What does a warehouseman do?
b. Why was Geoffrey Gray in a bad temper?
c. Did Mr Gray's boss ask him politely about the 20 tins of floor polish?
d. Would you have sacked the warehouseman?
e. If you were on the industrial tribunal, how would you decide the case?

2. [cassette icon]

Failing to obey the lights

AS Linda Duffield was driving home from her morning part-time job at a local architect's office, she saw a short queue of cars ahead of her at traffic lights.

Although red was showing, they were all gradually going forward across the junction – clearly the lights were jammed.

When it came to her turn, Linda looked carefully left, then right, hesitated (to give herself courage) and then slowly drove across – just as a policeman walked round the corner.

She ended up in the local magistrates' court charged with failing to obey the lights.

"But they were not working," said her lawyer. "You cannot 'fail to obey' something that is out of action."

"The lights were *not* out of action," insisted the prosecution. "They were jammed – and that's a very different thing. They *were* working – they were showing red."

a. Why were the cars in front of Linda all driving through the red light?
b. What would you have done in Linda's position?
c. What can a motorist do if (s)he doesn't want to drive through a light jammed at red?
d. If you had been the judge, would you have convicted Linda?

3. [cassette symbol]

The dog that came back from the dead

BLACKIE, the ugly little mongrel puppy Mrs Clarke had bought only five days before, was so ill that she thought he was dying.

The vet said the dog was suffering from a virus infection, and sadly Mrs Clarke decided to have Blackie put down to save him further suffering.

The vet agreed, Mrs Clarke paid the bill and left the dog at the vet's surgery, thinking she would never see him again.

Three months later she did see the mongrel again – at her local shopping centre, with a new name and a new owner. She recognized him at once – there couldn't be another dog as ugly as Blackie.

a. About how old do you think Blackie was when he got ill?
b. Why did Mrs Clarke ask the vet to put the puppy down?
c. The text says Mrs Clarke paid the bill. What do you think the bill was for?
d. What do you think were Mrs Clarke's feelings when she saw her dog again after three months?
e. How do you account for the fact that the dog was still alive and now belonged to someone else?
f. What would you have done if you had been in Mrs Clarke's position?

C Insight and practice

1. Conditional sentences: Make statements about the texts (→ G11)

a. if Geoffrey Gray / not be / tired and fed up / he / not lose / his temper
b. if he / not tell / his boss to "bugger off" / he / not be / dismissed
c. if Mrs Duffield / not drive / through the red lights / the policeman / not book / her
d. if the policeman / not see / her / she / not end up / in court
e. if Mrs Clarke / not think / the dog was dying / she / not ask / the vet to put him down
f. if the vet / put / Blackie down / Mrs Clarke / never see / him again

2. Pair work: Tag questions and short answers

> Mrs Duffield / be / on her way home
> A Mrs Duffield was on her way home, wasn't she?
> B Yes, she was.

a. the lights / be / showing red
b. Mrs Duffield / drive / across the lights
c. she / be / charged with failing to obey the lights
d. you / not have / to obey something that's out of action
e. Mr Gray / work / for the company for two years
f. it / not be / fair to dismiss him
g. Mrs Clarke / want / to save her dog further suffering
h. the vet / agree / to put him down
i. Mrs Clarke / think / she / never see / the dog again

3. Complete the text, putting in the correct forms of the verbs in brackets

The tribunal's decision

AFTER (hear) warehouseman Geoffrey Gray and the company's managing director, David Johnson, the industrial tribunal (decide) that Mr Gray (unfairly dismiss).

Under pressure at his work Mr Gray (use) language he shouldn't (use). It (be) a case for a warning and an apology but not for dismissal.

Mr Gray (award) £2,292 in compensation.

After the hearing Mr Johnson said: "It's not every day that a man (give) near two-and-a-half grand for (tell) the boss (bugger off). If anyone else (do) the same thing, I (sack) them, even though I can't afford it."

Mr Gray said: "Under the same circumstances, I (do) the same thing again. When there (be) a lot of men together, there's always a lot of (swear)."

Transfer

D

Role play: Arguing with somebody

a. You are Linda Duffield, who has just driven across the red light. A policeman (another student) wants to book you. Argue with him.

b. You are Mrs Clarke, who saw her dog Blackie at the shopping centre. Telephone the vet, Mr Shinton (another student), to ask what he did with the dog after you left it with him. (In fact, Mr Shinton's assistant liked the dog so much that she asked the vet to give him to her so she could try and save him.) Tell the vet how you feel about what he did.

c. The managing director (one student) wants to sack warehouseman Geoffrey Gray (another student) for swearing at his boss. Mr Gray defends himself and offers to apologize.

"Why don't you do something useful – like arresting a few detectives?"

Read the words in this square – across and down – in the right order to form an English proverb.

■	T	H	A	T
W	E	L	L	■
W	E	L	L	■
■	N	■	■	■
■	D	■	■	■
I	S	■	■	■

The world: political and communications

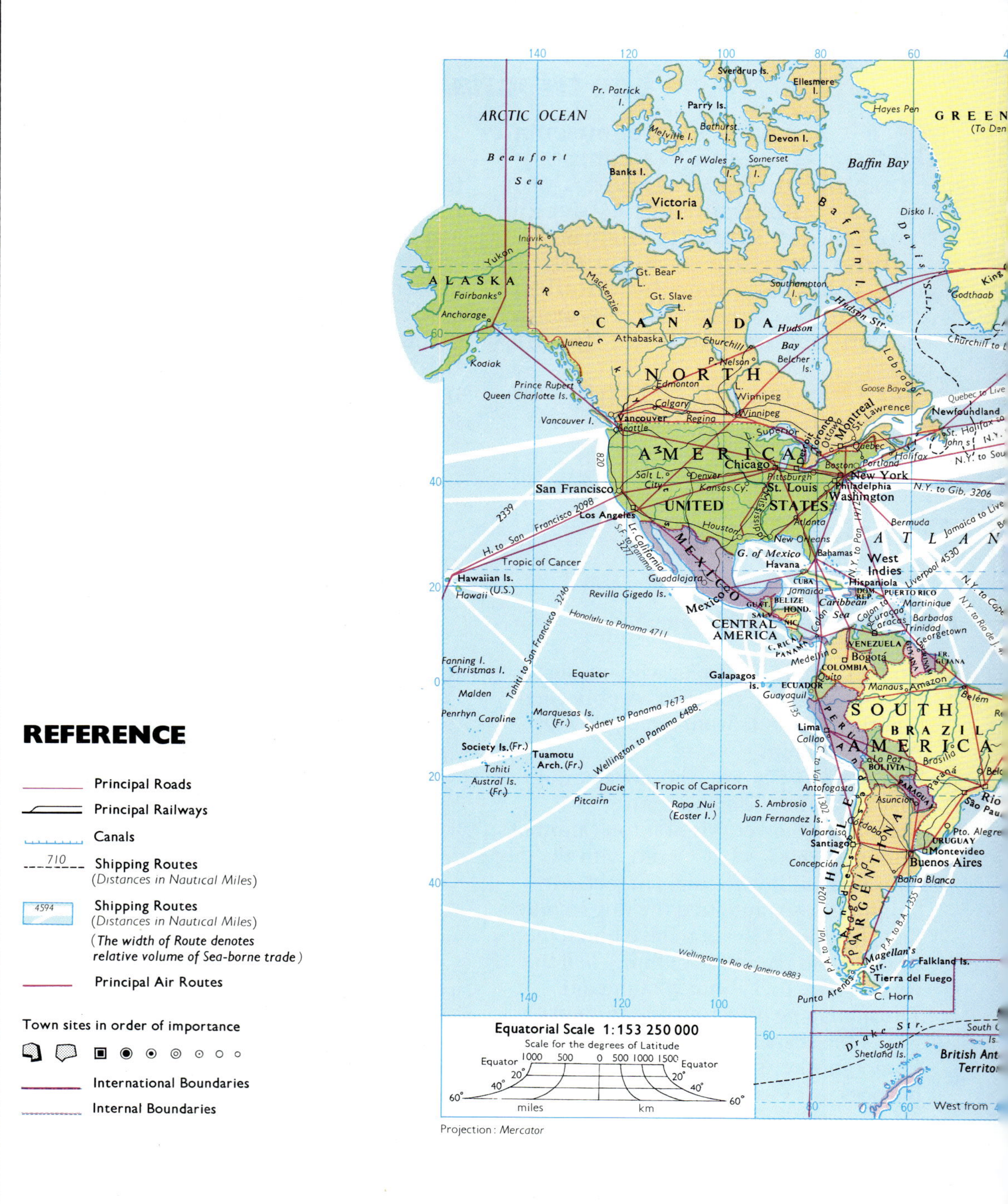

Spitsbergen (Norwegian)
A R C T I C O C E A N
C. Chelyuskin
Taimyr Pen.
New Siberian Is.
Laptev Sea
E. Siberian Sea
Lyakhov Is.
Wrangel I.
Bear I. (Norwegian)
Barents Sea
Novaya Zemlya
Kara Sea
Nordvik
Jan Mayen (Norwegian)
North C.
Murmansk
Kolguyev
Igarka
Verkhoyansk
Norwegian Sea
Arctic Circle
Arkhangelsk
Salekhard
Siberia
Lena
Ob
Yenisey
UNION OF SOVIET SOCIALIST REPUBLICS
Yakutsk
Stanovoy Mts.
Magadan
Okhotsk
Bering Sea
FINLAND
SWEDEN
NORWAY
Helsinki
Stockholm
Oslo
Leningrad
Gorki
Perm
Sverdlovsk
Ural Mts.
Tomsk
Krasnoyarsk
Kamchatka
Sea of Okhotsk
Komandorskiye Is.
Aleutian Is.
North Sea
Glasgow
DEN.
Copenhagen
Baltic Sea
Kazan
Kuybyshev
Chelyabinsk
Omsk
Novosibirsk
Irkutsk
L. Baikal
Yablonovyy Mts.
Petropavlovsk
London
Berlin
Warsaw
POLAND
Moscow
Volga
Orenburg
Karaganda
Chita
Sakhalin
Amur
Paris
FRANCE
Vienna
CZ.
Kiev
Kharkov
EUROPE
ASIA
L. Balkhash
MONGOLIA
Ulan-Bator
Manchuria
Harbin
Khabarovsk
Kuril Is.
Odessa
ROM.
BULG.
Black Sea
Caucasus
Caspian Sea
Aral
Tashkent
Tien Shan
Urumchi
Alma Ata
Gobi
Inner Mongolia
Shenyang
Vladivostok
Hokkaido
SPAIN
Madrid
Sardinia
ITALY
Rome
Istanbul
Ankara
Baku
Ashkhabad
Samarkand
Turkistan
Sinkiang-Uigur
Peking
Tientsin
KOREA
Sea of Japan
JAPAN
Tokyo
Yokohama
Yokohama to Victoria 4200
To San Francisco 4536
Mediterranean Sea
GREECE
Athens
TURKEY
Sicily
CYPRUS
SYRIA
Beirut
Tehran
IRAN (PERSIA)
AFGHANISTAN
Kabul
Lahore
CHINA
Kun Lun
Tibet
Mt. Everest
Lhasa
Sian
Hwang-ho
Seoul
Kitakyushu
Kyoto
Osaka
Yokohama to Honolulu 3379
Tunis
TUNISIA
Tripoli
Algiers
Alexandria
Baghdad
IRAQ
Jerusalem
JORDAN
Basra
PAKISTAN
Delhi
Himalaya
NEPAL
Chungking
Nanking
Shanghai
Wuhan
Yangtze-Kiang
Ryukyu Is.
Bonin Is.
ALGERIA
LIBYA
Cairo
EGYPT
Suez
SAUDI ARABIA
Mecca
U.A.E.
Karachi
INDIA
Calcutta
Canton
TAIWAN
Hong Kong
P A C I F I C
Tropic of Cancer
Sahara
Nile
Red Sea
Bombay
Arabian Sea
BURMA
Rangoon
Mariana Is. (US Tr. Terr.)
Wake I. (U.S.)
MALI
NIGER
Khartoum
SUDAN
YEMEN
SOUTH YEMEN
OMAN
B. of Bengal
Hyderabad
THAILAND
VIETNAM
Manila
Guam
International Date Line
CHAD
AFRICA
Addis Ababa
ETHIOPIA
SOMALI REP.
Socotra
Ras Asir
Lakshadweep Is.
Madras
Andaman Is.
Nicobar Is.
Bangkok
CAM.
Ho Chi Minh City
S. China Sea
PHILIPPINES
Caroline Is. (US. Trust Terr.)
Marshall Is. (US. Trust Terr.)
NIGERIA
Ibadan
GHANA
Accra
Lagos
CENTRAL AFRICA
CAMEROUN
SRI LANKA
Colombo
Maldive Is.
MALAYSIA
SABAH
SARAWAK
Singapore
Borneo
East Indies
Halmahera
Admiralty Is.
O C E A N
Kiribati
Bioko
GABON
CONGO
ZAÏRE
Zaire
KENYA
Nairobi
Mogadishu
Equator
Sumatra
INDONESIA
Celebes
Bismarck Arch.
WEST IRIAN
NEW GUINEA
PAPUA NEW GUINEA
Solomon Is.
Nauru
Tuvalu
Victoria
Mombasa
TANZANIA
Dar es Salaam
Amirante Is.
Seychelles
INDIAN
Chagos Arch.
Cocos or Keeling Is.
Jakarta
Java
Christmas I.
Timor
Timor Sea
Thursday I.
Port Moresby
Louisiade Arch.
Coral Sea
Benguela
ANGOLA
ZAMBIA
MALAWI
MOZAMBIQUE
Comoro Is.
Mauritius to Colombo
Darwin
Vanuatu
Fiji Is.
Suva
Southampton to Cape Town 5947
Salisbury
ZIMB.
Beira
MADAGASCAR
Antananarivo
OCEAN
Colombo to Fremantle 3120
Townsville
New Caledonia
Loyalty Is.
NAMIBIA
BOTSWANA
Kalahari
SOUTH WEST AFRICA
Réunion (Fr.)
Mauritius
Tropic of Capricorn
Alice Springs
Rockhampton
AUSTRALIA
L. Eyre
Brisbane
Sydney to Suva 1835
Norfolk I.
Maputo
Johannesburg
Drakensberg
Durban
SOUTH AFRICA
Fremantle
Perth
Sydney
Canberra
Kermadec Is.
A. to S. 1140
Cape Town
C. of Good Hope
Elizabeth
Cape Town to Melbourne 5814 Hobart 5838
F. to Adelaide 1353
Adelaide
Murray
Melbourne
Tasman Sea
North C.
Auckland
NEW ZEALAND
North I.
Wellington
Tasmania
Hobart
Christchurch
South I.
Stewart I.
Antipodes
Pr. Edward Is.
Crozet Is. (Fr.)
Kerguelen (Fr.)
Heard I.
Auckland I.
Bouvet Is.
Macquarie I.
Seas closed by Ice part of the year
SOUTHERN OCEAN
Norwegian Dependency
Australian Dependency
Fr. Dep.
Australian Dependency
Ross Dependency
Antarctic Circle
100 East from Greenwich

Wörterverzeichnis nach Units

Unit 1

1A	classroom ['klɑ:srʊm]	Klassenzimmer; Klasse
	opinion poll [ə'pɪnjən pəʊl]	Meinungsumfrage
	choose [tʃu:z] – chose [tʃəʊz] – chosen ['tʃəʊzn]	(aus)wählen – (aus)wählte – (aus)gewählt
	note something down ['nəʊt 'daʊn]	sich etw. notieren
	afterwards ['ɑ:ftəwədz]	danach; anschließend; nachher
	pollster ['pəʊlstə]	Meinungsforscher(in)
	report findings to someone [rɪ'pɔ:t]	jem. Ergebnisse mitteilen
	ship [ʃɪp]	Schiff
	go on separate holidays ['seprət]	("auf getrennte Urlaube gehen") getrennt Urlaub machen
	consider something the best place [kən'sɪdə]	etw. für den besten Ort halten / als den besten Ort ansehen
	caravan ['kærəvæn]	(BE) Wohnwagen
	tent [tent]	Zelt
	pick raspberries ['rɑ:zbrɪz]	Himbeeren pflücken
	pony trekking ['pəʊnɪ trekɪŋ]	Reitferien mit Pony
	put up a tent ['pʊt ʌp ə 'tent]	ein Zelt aufbauen/aufstellen/aufschlagen
1B	chat [tʃæt]	Unterhaltung; Plauderei
	solid-gold sunglasses ['sɒlɪd-'gəʊld]	Sonnenbrille(n) aus massivem Gold
	can you imagine anyone buying sunglasses for £1,100? [ɪ'mædʒɪn]	kannst du dir vorstellen, daß jem. eine Sonnenbrille für 1.100 Pfund kauft?
	mad [mæd]	verrückt
	posh [pɒʃ]	(piek)fein; vornehm
	if I had £1,100 to spare [speə]	wenn ich 1.100 Pfund übrig hätte
	I'd rather buy something else [els]	ich würde lieber etw. anderes kaufen
	darn [dɑ:n]	verdammt; verflixt
	weather forecast ['weðə fɔ:kɑ:st]	Wettervorhersage
	spread [spred] – spread – spread	(sich) ausbreiten – ausbreitete – ausgebreitet
	blasted winter! ['blɑ:stɪd 'wɪntə]	verdammter Winter!
	29 degrees and sunny [dɪ'gri:z]	29 Grad und sonnig
	nor am/can/would I ['nɔ:r əm 'aɪ]	ich auch nicht
	go to Australia just like that [ɒ'streɪljə]	einfach so nach Australien fahren
	fair [feə]	(Wetter:) heiter, schön
	the relationship between them [rɪ'leɪʃnʃɪp]	die Beziehung zwischen ihnen
	take place [teɪk 'pleɪs]	stattfinden
	licensed ['laɪsənst]	(Gastwirtschaft, Hotel etc.:) mit Konzession zum Ausschank/Verkauf von alkoholischen Getränken
	harbour ['hɑ:bə]	Hafen
	in own grounds [graʊndz]	auf eigenem Grundstück/Gelände
	TV lounge [ti:'vi: laʊnʒ]	Fernsehraum, -zimmer
	ideal [aɪ'dɪəl]	ideal
	free baby-sitting service	kostenloser Babysitter-Service/Dienst
	reasonable rates ['ri:znəbl 'reɪts]	("vernünftige", "angemessene") günstige Preise
	well-equipped [wel-ɪ'kwɪpt]	gut ausgestattet
	unspoiled ['ʌn'spɔɪlt]	unverdorben
	peaceful ['pi:sfʊl]	friedlich
	cottage ['kɒtɪdʒ]	(kleines) (Land-/Sommer- etc.)Haus
	accept something [ək'sept]	etw. akzeptieren/annehmen/hinnehmen
	give full particulars [pə'tɪkjʊləz]	genaue Angaben machen

	Ave. (= Avenue) ['ævənju:]	Straße; Allee
	time share ['taɪm ʃeə]	(Zeitbruchteilseigentum an Gebäuden etc.)
	buy a share ['baɪ ə 'ʃeə]	einen Anteil / eine Beteiligung erwerben
	the proceeds of the sale ['prəʊsi:dz]	der Erlös aus dem Verkauf
	s.a.e. (= stamped addressed envelope) ['stæmpt ə'drest 'envələʊp]	("frankierter adressierter Umschlag") frankierter Rückumschlag
	development [dɪ'veləpmənt]	Entwicklung
	a wise investment [ɪn'vestmənt]	eine kluge Investition/Kapitalanlage
	property ['prɒpətɪ]	Grundstück; Gebäude; Liegenschaft
	a particular week [pə'tɪkjʊlə]	eine bestimmte Woche
	sender ['sendə]	Absender(in)
	on the back [bæk]	auf der Rückseite
	break [breɪk] – broke [brəʊk] – broken ['brəʊkən]	(Sturm:) losbrechen – losbrach – losgebrochen
	dogs' home ['dɒgz həʊm]	Hundeasyl
	at reduced prices [rɪ'dju:st]	zu reduzierten/herabgesetzten Preisen
	camping area ['kæmpɪŋ eərɪə]	Campingplatz
	site [saɪt]	Platz; Stelle
1C	ad(vertisement) [æd/əd'vɜ:tɪsmənt]	Anzeige; Annonce; Inserat
	freeze [fri:z] – froze [frəʊz] – frozen ['frəʊzn]	frieren – fror – gefroren
	sail to New York [seɪl]	(mit dem Schiff) nach New York fahren
1D	advert(isement) ['ædvɜ:t]	Anzeige; Annonce; Inserat
	include something [ɪn'klu:d]	etw. einschließen/einbeziehen
	require something [rɪ'kwaɪə]	etw. benötigen/brauchen
	adult ['ædʌlt]	Erwachsene(r)
	shower ['ʃaʊə]	Dusche; Brause
	deposit [dɪ'pɒzɪt]	Anzahlung; Kaution
	reduction [rɪ'dʌkʃn]	Ermäßigung; (Preis-)Nachlaß
	brochure ['brəʊʃə]	Prospekt; Broschüre
	requirements [rɪ'kwaɪəmənts]	Bedürfnisse; Ansprüche; Erfordernisse; Wünsche
	tennis court ['tenɪs kɔ:t]	Tennisplatz
	ride [raɪd] – rode [rəʊd] – ridden ['rɪdn]	reiten – ritt – geritten
	the pros and cons ['prəʊz n 'kɒnz]	das Für und Wider; das Pro und Kontra
	protect against something [prə'tekt]	gegen etw. (be)schützen
	an empty house/glass ['emtɪ]	ein leeres Haus/Glas
	an unoccupied house [ʌn'ɒkjʊpaɪd]	ein leerstehendes/unbewohntes Haus
	burglar ['bɜ:glə]	Einbrecher(in)
	tied down to a particular time [taɪd]	an eine bestimmte Zeit gebunden; auf eine bestimmte Zeit festgelegt
	unless (that happens) [ən'les]	wenn (das) nicht (geschieht)
	exchange [ɪks'tʃeɪnʒ]	(Aus-)Tausch
	make arrangements with somebody [ə'reɪnʒmənts]	mit jem. Vereinbarungen/Absprachen treffen
	share something with someone [ʃeə]	etw. mit jem. teilen / gemeinsam haben
	with up to 51 people ['pi:pl]	mit bis zu 51 Leuten
	mood [mu:d]	Stimmung

Unit 2

2A	suspect something [sə'spekt]	etw. argwöhnen/vermuten
	motorist ['məʊtərɪst]	Kraft-/Autofahrer(in)
	drink [drɪŋk] – drank [dræŋk] – drunk [drʌŋk]	trinken – trank – getrunken
	catch [kætʃ] – caught [kɔ:t] – caught	erwischen – erwischte – erwischt

	at the wheel [wi:l]	am ("Rad") Steuer
	drug [drʌg]	Medikament; Arzneimittel; Droge
	sober ['səʊbə]	nüchtern
	when police see a car going from side to side [pə'li:s]	wenn Polizisten ein Auto zickzack fahren sehen
	freeway ['fri:weɪ]	(AE u. Austral.) Autobahn, Schnellstraße
	sway [sweɪ]	schwanken
	a great success [sək'ses]	ein großer Erfolg
	he was disqualified from driving [dɪs'kwɒlɪfaɪd]	ihm wurde der Führerschein entzogen
	blow in(to) the bag [bləʊ]	in die Tüte blasen
	blood test ['blʌd test]	Blutprobe
	jail sentence ['dʒeɪl sentəns]	Gefängnisstrafe
	give a sample of his breath [breθ]	"eine Probe seines Atems geben"
	test something [test]	etw. prüfen/testen/untersuchen
	fine [faɪn]	Geldstrafe; Bußgeld
	he's drunk [drʌŋk]	er ist betrunken
	(driving) licence ['laɪsəns]	Führerschein
	suffer ['sʌfə]	(er)leiden
	successful [sək'sesfʊl]	erfolgreich
2B	refuse to do something [rɪ'fju:z]	sich weigern, etw. zu tun
	he was fined $300 [faɪnd]	er mußte ein Bußgeld von 300 Dollar zahlen
	self-employed ['self-ɪm'plɔɪd]	selbständig; freischaffend; freiberuflich
	builder ['bɪldə]	Bauunternehmer(in)
	he pleaded not guilty ['pli:dɪd . . . 'gɪltɪ]	er bekannte sich nicht schuldig
	under the influence of alcohol ['ɪnflʊəns əv 'ælkəhɒl]	unter dem Einfluß von Alkohol / Alkoholeinfluß
	constable ['kʌnstəbl]	(Polizei-)Hauptwachtmeister
	in court [kɔ:t]	vor Gericht
	eastern ['i:stən]	östlich
	get out of the car [get 'aʊt]	aus dem Auto aussteigen
	forward ['fɔ:wəd]	vorwärts; nach vorn
	hold up [həʊld] – held up [held] – held up	hochhalten – hochhielt – hochgehalten
	get something out ['get . . . 'aʊt]	etw. herausholen/herausnehmen
	drop something on the road [rəʊd]	etw. auf die Straße fallen lassen
	analysis [ə'næləsɪs]	Analyse; Untersuchung
	magistrates' court ['mædʒɪstreɪts kɔ:t]	Magistratsgericht (= unterste Instanz der Strafgerichtsbarkeit, meist mit ehrenamtl. Friedensrichtern)
	charge [tʃɑ:dʒ]	Anklage
	defendant [dɪ'fendənt]	Angeklagte(r)
	lawyer ['lɔɪə]	(Rechts-)Anwalt, Anwältin
	the prosecution [prɒsɪ'kju:ʃn]	die (Vertreter der) Anklage; die Staatsanwaltschaft
	witness ['wɪtnɪs]	Zeuge, Zeugin
	and not too crowded either ['kraʊdɪd]	und auch nicht (all)zu überfüllt/voll
	a half of lager [ə 'hɑ:f əv 'lɑ:gə]	ein halbes (Pint) Helles
	cheers! [tʃɪəz]	prost! / prosit! / zum Wohl!
	let's have another! [ə'nʌðə]	laß(t) uns noch einen trinken!
	drink over the limit ['lɪmɪt]	"über das Limit" / mehr als erlaubt trinken
	that didn't bother him too much ['bɒðə]	das hat ihm nicht allzuviel ausgemacht
	oh Lord! [lɔ:d]	ach, du lieber Gott/Himmel!
	you can't risk it [rɪsk]	man kann es nicht riskieren

	as a salesman you're finished if . . . ['fɪnɪʃt]	als (Handlungs-)Reisender/Reisevertreter ist man erledigt, wenn . . .
	a news item ['nju:z aɪtəm]	eine Nachricht
	tragic end of a drinking party ['trædʒɪk]	tragisches Ende eines Trinkgelages
	he celebrated his 21st birthday ['selɪbreɪtɪd]	er feierte seinen 21. Geburtstag
	crash head-on into another car [kræʃ]	mit einem anderen Wagen frontal zusammenstoßen
	they were killed outright [aʊt'raɪt]	sie waren sofort tot
	real earnings increased [ɪn'kri:st]	die Realeinkommen nahmen zu
	relatively cheaper ['relətɪvlɪ]	relativ/verhältnismäßig billiger
	a drop in prices ['praɪsɪz]	ein Preisrückgang/-sturz
	without regret [rɪ'gret]	ohne Bedauern/Reue
	develop a drug [dɪ'veləp ə 'drʌg]	ein Arzneimittel entwickeln
	sober up ['səʊbər 'ʌp]	nüchtern werden
	stuff [stʌf]	Stoff; Zeug
	wait for their heads to clear [klɪə]	warten darauf, daß der Kopf klar wird
	prevent an accident [prɪ'vent]	einen Unfall verhindern
	nasty ['nɑ:stɪ]	gemein; bösartig; unangenehm
	there's so much shouting and fighting	es gibt soviel Geschrei und Zank
	hear [hɪə] – heard [hɜ:d] – heard	hören – hörte – gehört
	fight [faɪt]	Streit; Auseinandersetzung
	get divorced [dɪ'vɔ:st]	sich scheiden lassen
	I'm ashamed [ə'ʃeɪmd]	ich schäme mich
	we're having friends over [frendz]	wir haben Freunde eingeladen
	talk sense into someone [sens]	jem. zur Vernunft bringen / gut zureden
	make sure [meɪk 'ʃʊə]	sich vergewissern; darauf achten
	a happy marriage ['mærɪdʒ]	eine glückliche Ehe
2C	the house next to ours [haʊs]	das Haus neben unserem
2D	drink-driver [drɪŋk-'draɪvə]	betrunkene(r) Autofahrer(in)
	drink-driving [drɪŋk-'draɪvɪŋ]	Trunkenheit am Steuer
	increase at the same rate as [ɪn'kri:s]	im gleichen/selben Maß zunehmen/steigen wie
	the blood-alcohol limit ['blʌd-ælkəhɒl]	das Blutalkohol-Limit
	lower the limit ['ləʊə]	das Limit senken/herabsetzen
	the manufacture of alcoholic drinks [mænjʊ'fæktʃər əv ælkə'hɒlɪk 'drɪŋks]	die Herstellung alkoholischer Getränke
	forbid [fə'bɪd] – forbade [fə'bæd] – forbidden	verbieten – verbot – verboten
	Scotch (whisky) ['skɒtʃ 'wɪskɪ]	schottischer Whisky
	boast [bəʊst]	prahlen; sich rühmen

Unit 3

3A	otherwise ['ʌðəwaɪz]	andernfalls; sonst
	I can't sew [səʊ]	ich kann nicht nähen
3B	she's always on the ball [bɔ:l]	sie ist immer am Ball
	routine [ru:'ti:n]	Routine
	a (metal) claw [klɔ:]	eine (Metall-)Klaue
	above her head [ə'bʌv hə 'hed]	über ihrem Kopf
	pull a string ['pʊl ə 'strɪŋ]	an einer Schnur ziehen
	sit alongside [əlɒŋ'saɪd]	daneben sitzen
	look into the mirror ['mɪrə]	in den Spiegel sehen/gucken/schauen
	tape [teɪp]	(z. B. Klebe-, aber auch Ton-)Band
	stick [stɪk] – stuck [stʌk] – stuck	kleben – klebte – geklebt

horizontal(ly) [hɒrɪ'zɒntl(-əlɪ)]	horizontal; waagerecht
above/on the floor [flɔ:]	über/auf dem (Fuß-)Boden
the ball bounces to a point between the two lines ['baʊnsɪz]	der Ball springt bis zu einem Punkt zwischen den beiden Linien
it must not be passed for sale [pɑ:st]	er darf nicht für den Verkauf freigegeben werden
inspect something [ɪn'spekt]	etw. prüfen/kontrollieren
printing shop ['prɪntɪŋ ʃɒp]	Druckerei
it ends just after 5 a.m. [endz]	er hört kurz nach fünf (Uhr morgens) auf
he works nights [naɪts]	er arbeitet nachts
honestly ['ɒnɪstlɪ]	ehrlich (gesagt)
you get used to it ['ju:stʊ ɪt]	man gewöhnt sich daran
wake up [weɪk 'ʌp]	aufwachen
however [haʊ'evə]	(je)doch; aber
make a point of doing something [pɔɪnt]	Wert darauf legen / darauf bedacht sein, etw. zu tun
is he up yet? [jet]	ist er schon auf?
she makes her own way [hər 'əʊn 'weɪ]	sie schlägt sich selber durch / verdient sich ihren Lebensunterhalt selbst
vet's assistant ['vets ə'sɪstənt]	Tierarzthelfer(in)
Jobcentre ['dʒɒbsentə]	(BE) staatliche Arbeitsvermittlung
she had just two choices ['tʃɔɪsɪz]	sie hatte nur zwei (Wahl-)Möglichkeiten
dole [dəʊl]	(BE umgangssprachl.) Arbeitslosengeld, -hilfe
join a queue ['dʒɔɪn ə 'kju:]	sich (in einer Schlange) anstellen
talent ['tælənt]	Begabung; Talent
design dresses [dɪ'zaɪn 'dresɪz]	Kleider entwerfen
she realized ['rɪəlaɪzd]	sie erkannte; es wurde ihr klar
sewing machine ['səʊɪŋ məʃi:n]	Nähmaschine
remnants of material picked up cheaply at local markets ['remnənts əv mə'tɪərɪəl]	Stoffreste, die sie billig auf dortigen/hiesigen Märkten bekommen hatte
clothes that appeal to youngsters [kləʊðz]	Kleider/Sachen, die Jugendlichen gefallen
it was heavy going at first ['hevɪ 'gəʊɪŋ]	zuerst tat sie sich schwer
her efforts began to pay off ['efəts]	ihre Anstrengungen begannen sich auszuzahlen
put on a fashion show ['fæʃn ʃəʊ]	eine Mode(n)schau veranstalten
I'm willing to work ['wɪlɪŋ]	ich bin bereit/gewillt zu arbeiten
skilled or unskilled workers [skɪld]	gelernte Arbeiter / Facharbeiter oder ungelernte Arbeiter
coloured ['kʌləd]	(auch Rasse:) farbig
skill [skɪl]	Fähigkeit; Fertigkeit
(un)limited ['lɪmɪtɪd]	(un)begrenzt
single ['sɪŋgl]	ledig; unverheiratet
preferably mornings ['prefrəblɪ]	vorzugsweise / am liebsten / wenn möglich morgens / vormittags
do translations [træns'leɪʃnz]	Übersetzungen anfertigen/machen
teach [ti:tʃ] – taught [tɔ:t] – taught	unterrichten – unterrichtete – unterrichtet
prepare simple meals [prɪ'peə]	einfache Mahlzeiten zubereiten
lonely ['ləʊnlɪ]	einsam
sing folk songs ['fəʊk sɒŋz]	Volkslieder singen
act [ækt]	(Theater) spielen; schauspielern
extra ['ekstrə]	Statist(in); Komparse, Komparsin
tidy ['taɪdɪ]	ordentlich; gepflegt
I'm prepared to work hard [hɑ:d]	ich bin bereit, hart zu arbeiten
reasonably good-looking ['ri:znəblɪ]	recht/leidlich gutaussehend
I'm running out of money ['mʌnɪ]	mir geht das Geld aus

	without delay [dɪ'leɪ]	ohne Verzögerung; unverzüglich
	yours truly ['jɔːz 'truːlɪ]	(Briefschluß:) mit freundlichen Grüßen / hochachtungsvoll
	demonstrate something ['demənstreɪt]	etw. zeigen/demonstrieren/vorführen
	agency ['eɪdʒənsɪ]	Agentur; Vermittlung
	train someone for an occupation [ɒkjʊ'peɪʃn]	jem. für einen Beruf ausbilden
	mouse [maʊs] – mice [maɪs]	Maus – Mäuse
	actress ['æktrɪs]	Schauspielerin
	actor ['æktə]	Schauspieler
	her acting career ['æktɪŋ kə'rɪə]	ihre Schauspielkarriere
	tie a parcel up ['taɪ ə 'pɑːsl ʌp]	ein Paket verschnüren
3C	expand a sentence [ɪk'spænd]	einen Satz erweitern
	a blood-alcohol content of 0.18 per cent ['kɒntent]	ein Blutalkoholgehalt von 1,8‰
3D	consider Jack [kən'sɪdə]	denken Sie an Jack
	she's on her own [əʊn]	sie ist allein/selbständig
	stay alive ['steɪ ə'laɪv]	am Leben bleiben
	mention something ['menʃn]	etw. erwähnen

Unit 4

4A	electric shaver [ɪ'lektrɪk 'ʃeɪvə]	Elektrorasierer; Trockenrasierer
	they exchanged it for a new one [ɪks'tʃeɪnʒd]	sie tauschten es gegen ein neues um
	send something in for repair [rɪ'peə]	etw. zur Reparatur einschicken
	no wonder ['wʌndə]	kein Wunder; nicht verwunderlich
	it tasted strange somehow ['teɪstɪd 'streɪnʒ]	er schmeckte irgendwie seltsam/sonderbar/merkwürdig
	mouldy ['məʊldɪ]	verschimmelt; schimmelig
	discover something [dɪ'skʌvə]	etw. entdecken/herausfinden/feststellen
	she looked more closely ['kləʊslɪ]	sie sah/schaute genauer hin
	when she showed it to an attendant [ə'tendənt]	als sie ihn/es einem Angestellten zeigte
	he just shrugged [ʃrʌgd]	er zuckte nur die / mit den Achseln
	replacement [rɪ'pleɪsmənt]	Ersatz
	satisfy someone ['sætɪsfaɪ]	jem. befriedigen/zufriedenstellen
	at the dry-cleaner's [draɪ-'kliːnəz]	in der (chem.) Reinigung
	complaint [kəm'pleɪnt]	Beschwerde; Reklamation
	length [leŋθ]	Länge
	floor-length curtains ['flɔː-leŋθ 'kɜːtnz]	bodenlange / bis auf den Boden reichende Vorhänge
	ruin something ['rʊɪn]	etw. ruinieren/verderben/zerstören
	insist on/that [ɪn'sɪst]	bestehen auf / darauf bestehen, daß
	I'm terribly sorry ['terəblɪ 'sɒrɪ]	es tut mir schrecklich/furchtbar leid
	replace something [rɪ'pleɪs]	etw. ersetzen
	demand something/that [dɪ'mɑːnd]	etw. verlangen / verlangen, daß
4B	complain to somebody about something	sich bei jem. über etw. beschweren
	psychologist [saɪ'kɒlədʒɪst]	Psychologe, Psychologin
	aggressive [ə'gresɪv]	aggressiv; angriffslustig
	get results [rɪ'zʌlts]	Resultate erzielen
	her newly bought jeans ['njuːlɪ bɔːt]	ihre gerade gekauften Jeans
	split at the seams (split – split – split) [siːmz]	an den Nähten aufplatzen
	point out a fault [fɔːlt]	auf einen Mangel hinweisen
	method ['meθəd]	Methode
	he stood on a chair ['stʊd ɒn ə 'tʃeə]	er stellte sich auf einen Stuhl

	shout [ʃaʊt]	rufen; schreien; brüllen
	rubbish ['rʌbɪʃ]	(eigentlich:) Abfall, Müll; (übertr.:) Plunder, Mist, Blödsinn
	a new pair of jeans ['peər əv 'dʒi:nz]	eine neue Jeanshose
	speak loudly ['spi:k 'laʊdlɪ]	laut sprechen
	mean business ['bɪznɪs]	es ernst meinen
	invitation [ɪnvɪ'teɪʃn]	Einladung; Aufforderung
	consumer protection [kən'sju:mə prə'tekʃn]	Verbraucherschutz
	specialist ['speʃəlɪst]	Spezialist(in)
	cancel something by mistake ['kænsl]	etw. irrtümlich / aus Versehen rückgängig machen / streichen / stornieren
	manager ['mænɪdʒə]	Geschäftsführer
	undress [ʌn'dres]	sich ausziehen/entkleiden
	lobby ['lɒbɪ]	(Hotel-)Halle; Eingangshalle
	he put on his pyjamas [pə'dʒɑ:məz]	er zog seinen Schlafanzug/Pyjama an
	sofa ['səʊfə]	Sofa
	he immediately got a room [ɪ'mi:djətlɪ]	er bekam sofort ein Zimmer
	organization [ɔ:gənaɪ'zeɪʃn]	Organisation; Unternehmen
	hardly ever ['hɑ:dlɪ 'evə]	kaum je(mals); fast nie
	employee [emplɔɪ'i:]	Arbeitnehmer(in); Angestellte(r)
	I'll sort it out straight away [streɪt]	ich werde es sofort in Ordnung bringen
	the cause of the trouble [kɔ:z]	die Ursache des Problems
	beyond the control [bɪ'jɒnd ðə kən'trəʊl]	jenseits/außerhalb der Kontrolle
	deal with a person [di:l]	mit jem. zu tun haben
	the breakdown of a lorry ['lɒrɪ]	die Panne an einem Lastwagen/Lkw
	computer [kəm'pju:tə]	Computer
	the rail strike ['reɪl straɪk]	der Eisenbahn(er)streik
	Middle East ['mɪdl 'i:st]	("Mittlerer", dt. aber:) Naher Osten
	advice [əd'vaɪs]	(ein) Rat(schlag); Ratschläge
	never show any interest in/for ['ɪntrəst]	zeigen Sie nie Interesse an/für
	sympathy ['sɪmpəθɪ]	Mitgefühl; Verständnis
	explanation [eksplə'neɪʃn]	Erklärung
	interrupt someone [ɪntə'rʌpt]	jem. unterbrechen
	opponent [ə'pəʊnənt]	Gegner(in)
	attack someone [ə'tæk]	jem. angreifen
	I don't care [keə]	es ist mir egal/gleichgültig/Wurscht
	I'm holding you responsible [rɪ'spɒnsəbl]	ich mache Sie verantwortlich
	I'll bring it to the attention of your head office ['hed 'ɒfɪs]	ich werde das Ihrer Zentrale zur Kenntnis bringen
	threaten to do something ['θretn]	(an)drohen, etw. zu tun
	cause trouble ['kɔ:z 'trʌbl]	Ärger verursachen; Schwierigkeiten bereiten
	strap [stræp]	Riemen; (Uhr:) Band
	watch [wɒtʃ]	(Armband-/Taschen-)Uhr
4C	the underlined nouns [naʊnz]	die unterstrichenen Substantive/Hauptwörter
	we discussed the matter [dɪ'skʌst]	wir diskutierten (über) die Angelegenheit/Sache
	the woman whose daughter had bought the jeans	die Frau, deren Tochter die Jeans gekauft hatte
	condition(al sentence) [kən'dɪʃn]	Bedingung(ssatz)
	World Cup ['wɜ:ld 'kʌp]	("Weltpokal") Fußballweltmeisterschaft
	dress designer ['dres dɪzaɪnə]	Modezeichner(in)
4D	complain by letter/phone [kəm'pleɪn]	sich brieflich/telefonisch beschweren
	travel firm ['trævl fɜ:m]	Reiseunternehmen
	dust [dʌst]	Staub

inconvenience [ɪnkən'vi:njəns]	Unannehmlichkeit(en); Unbequemlichkeit
building rubble ['bɪldɪŋ rʌbl]	Bauschutt
plastic bottles ['plæstɪk 'bɒtlz]	Plastik-/Kunststoff-Flaschen
tin [tɪn]	(Konserven-)Büchse, Dose
hardly got any sleep ['hɑ:dlɪ]	bekam kaum Schlaf
just a stone's throw away ['stəʊnz θrəʊ]	nur einen Steinwurf entfernt
exorbitant prices [ɪg'zɔ:bɪtənt]	horrende/unverschämte Preise
a Coke [kəʊk]	eine (Coca-)Cola
lousy service ['laʊzɪ 'sɜ:vɪs]	miserabler Service
tour operator(s) ['tʊər ɒpəreɪtə(z)]	Reiseveranstalter
Ltd (= Limited) ['lɪmɪtɪd]	("begrenzt") (etwa:) mit beschränkter Haftung

Unit 5

5A	proverb ['prɒvɜ:b]	Sprichwort
	square [skweə]	Quadrat; Viereck
	in brackets ['brækɪts]	in Klammern
	cross off letters ['krɒs ɒf]	Buchstaben (an)streichen
	pop music ['pɒp mju:zɪk]	Popmusik
	useless things ['ju:sləs]	nutzlose/unnütze/unbrauchbare Dinge
	jacket ['dʒækɪt]	Jacke; Jackett
	a piece of cloth [klɒθ]	ein Stück Tuch/Stoff
	draw [drɔ:] – drew [dru:] – drawn [drɔ:n]	ziehen – zog – gezogen
	shut out the light ['ʃʌt aʊt]	das Licht ("ausschließen") nicht hereinlassen
	cotton ['kɒtn]	Baumwolle
	flat land ['flæt 'lænd]	flaches Land
	covered with sand ['kʌvəd wɪð 'sænd]	mit Sand bedeckt
	what's his salary? ['sælərɪ]	wie hoch ist sein Gehalt?
	producer [prə'dju:sə]	Hersteller; Produzent; Erzeuger
	the science of the human mind ['saɪəns]	die Wissenschaft von der menschlichen Psyche
	he knows a great deal [di:l]	er weiß eine ganze Menge
	nature ['neɪtʃə]	Wesen(sart); Natur
5B	raid [reɪd]	Überfall; Einbruch
	theft [θeft]	Diebstahl
	the City ['sɪtɪ]	die City (= Banken- u. Börsenviertel v. London)
	recently ['ri:sntlɪ]	in letzter Zeit
	transfer money [træns'fɜ:]	Geld überweisen
	account [ə'kaʊnt]	(Bank-)Konto
	there oughtn't to be too much cash lying around ['ɔ:tnt]	es sollte/dürfte (eigentlich) nicht allzu viel Bargeld herumliegen
	thief [θi:f] – thieves [θi:vz]	Dieb(in) – Diebe/Diebinnen
	strongroom ['strɒŋrʊm]	Stahlkammer; Tresor(raum)
	steal [sti:l] – stole [stəʊl] – stolen ['stəʊlən]	stehlen – stahl – gestohlen
	safe-deposit box ['seɪf-dɪpɒzɪt bɒks]	(Bank-)Schließfach; Banksafe; Schrankfach
	clean the boxes out [kli:n]	die Schließfächer ausräumen
	the bank officials ['bæŋk əfɪʃlz]	die Bankbeamten/Bankangestellten
	plenty of valuable things ['væljʊəbl]	eine Menge wertvoller Dinge
	jewels ['dʒu:əlz]	Juwelen; Edelsteine
	the international diamond trade ['daɪəmənd]	der internationale Diamantenhandel
	dealer ['di:lə]	Händler(in)
	among the customers [ə'mʌŋ]	unter den Kunden

	raid a bank ['reɪd ə 'bæŋk]	eine Bank überfallen
	robber ['rɒbə]	Räuber
	clever ['klevə]	geschickt; raffiniert; schlau
	point a gun at somebody [gʌn]	eine Schußwaffe/Pistole auf jem. richten
	get out of the way!	gehen Sie aus dem Weg!
	apparently [ə'pærəntlɪ]	anscheinend
	unlock the door [ʌn'lɒk]	die Tür aufschließen
	it appears [ə'pɪəz]	es scheint / hat den Anschein
	key [kiː]	Schlüssel
	smooth [smuːð]	glatt; reibungslos
	a professional job [prə'feʃnl]	ein professioneller Job
	obviously ['ɒbvɪəslɪ]	offensichtlich; offenbar
	no one noticed the theft ['nəʊtɪst]	niemand bemerkte den Diebstahl
	rob somebody [rɒb]	jem. berauben/ausrauben
	the lock is jammed [dʒæmd]	das Schloß klemmt
	engineer [enʒɪ'nɪə]	Techniker(in); Ingenieur(in)
	locksmith ['lɒksmɪθ]	Schlosser
	all their efforts failed ['efəts]	alle ihre Anstrengungen waren vergeblich/umsonst
	at long last [ət lɒŋ 'lɑːst]	schließlich und endlich
	make a decision [dɪ'sɪʒn]	eine Entscheidung treffen/fällen; sich entschließen
	beside the doors [bɪ'saɪd]	neben den Türen
	a hell of a job [hel]	*(hell = Hölle)* eine Wahnsinnsarbeit
	force the boxes open [fɔːs]	die Fächer aufbrechen
	valuables ['væljʊəblz]	Wertsachen; Wertgegenstände
	surely ['ʃʊəlɪ]	bestimmt; sicher
	they ought to have an alarm system [ə'lɑːm]	sie müßten/sollten (eigentlich) eine Alarmanlage haben
	a false alarm ['fɔːls ə'lɑːm]	ein falscher Alarm
	how much was missing? ['mɪsɪŋ]	wieviel fehlte?
	lock the door/box [dɔː]	die Tür / das Fach verschließen
	how can one prove one's loss? [pruːv]	wie kann man seinen Verlust beweisen?
	insure something (against theft) [ɪn'ʃʊə]	etw. (gegen Diebstahl) versichern
	reporter [rɪ'pɔːtə]	Reporter(in)
	particularly attractive [pə'tɪkjʊləlɪ]	besonders attraktiv
	closed-circuit television ['kləʊzd-sɜːkɪt]	interne Fernseh(überwachungs)anlage
5C	structure ['strʌktʃə]	Struktur
	keep something in a safe place	etw. an einem sicheren Ort aufbewahren
	the contents of the boxes ['kɒntents]	der Inhalt der Fächer
	amateurs and professionals ['æmətəz]	Amateure und Profis
	careless ['keələs]	nachlässig; unvorsichtig; leichtsinnig
	bank robbery ['bæŋk rɒbərɪ]	Bankraub
5D	interview somebody ['ɪntəvjuː]	jem. interviewen
	press conference ['pres kɒnfrəns]	Pressekonferenz
	news story ['njuːz stɔːrɪ]	(Zeitungs-)Bericht
	outline ['aʊtlaɪn]	Entwurf; Abriß
	gang [gæŋ]	(Verbrecher-)Bande
	the boxes contained jewels [kən'teɪnd]	die Fächer enthielten Juwelen
	they succeeded in opening the boxes [sək'siːdɪd]	es gelang ihnen, die Fächer zu öffnen

Unit 6

6A	season ['si:zn]	Jahreszeit
	take something along [teɪk . . . ə'lɒŋ]	etw. mitnehmen
	if you were to visit Alice Springs in July	wenn Sie Alice Springs im Juli besuchen sollten
	time zone ['taɪm zəʊn]	Zeitzone
	distance ['dɪstəns]	Entfernung
	maximum ['mæksɪməm]	Maximum; maximal; Höchst-
	daylight-saving time ['deɪlaɪt-seɪvɪŋ]	Sommerzeit
	a hill of bare stone [beə]	ein Berg aus kahlem/nacktem (Ge-)Stein
	the base is 8.8 kilometres around [beɪs]	der Sockel / die Grundfläche hat einen Umfang von 8,8 km
	the plains [pleɪnz]	das Flachland; die Ebene/Prärie
	at sunrise ['sʌnraɪz]	bei Sonnenaufgang
	at sunset ['sʌnset]	bei Sonnenuntergang
	climb a rock ['klaɪm ə 'rɒk]	einen Felsen besteigen; auf einen Felsen klettern
	enter a name ['entər ə 'neɪm]	einen Namen eintragen
	at the summit ['sʌmɪt]	auf dem Gipfel
	print [prɪnt]	drucken
6B	it's a pity ['pɪtɪ]	es ist schade
	I had to hurry ['hʌrɪ]	ich mußte mich beeilen
	at the bottom of the rock ['bɒtəm]	am Fuß des Felsens
	motel [məʊ'tel]	Motel
	congratulate somebody on something [kən'grætjʊleɪt]	jem. zu etw. gratulieren
	a fine effort ['efət]	eine gute/prima Leistung
	chap [tʃæp]	Kerl; Bursche; “Typ”
	print [prɪnt]	Abzug/Vergrößerung (eines Fotos)
	photograph ['fəʊtəgrɑ:f]	Fotografie; Aufnahme
	glory ['glɔ:rɪ]	Ehre; Ruhm; Stolz
	delightful [dɪ'laɪtfʊl]	reizend; entzückend; herrlich
	in your travels ['trævlz]	auf Ihren Reisen
	the outback ['aʊtbæk]	(Austral.) das Landesinnere, das Hinterland
	with kind regards ['kaɪnd rɪ'gɑ:dz]	mit freundlichen Grüßen
	roughly 50 kilometres ['rʌflɪ]	ungefähr 50 Kilometer
	cover 50 miles a day ['kʌvə]	pro Tag 50 Meilen zurücklegen
	mail run ['meɪl rʌn]	Postflug
	charter plane ['tʃɑ:tə pleɪn]	Charterflugzeug
	cattle station ['kætl steɪʃn]	(Austral.) Rinderfarm
	accompany somebody [ə'kʌmpənɪ]	jem. begleiten
	pilot ['paɪlət]	Pilot(in)
	bush fire ['bʊʃ faɪə]	Buschfeuer
	camel ['kæml]	Kamel
	go wild [gəʊ 'waɪld]	(“wild”) frei herumlaufen; verwildern
	homestead ['həʊmsted]	Gehöft; (Austral. auch) Hauptgebäude auf *sheep/ cattle station*
	get stuck [get 'stʌk]	steckenbleiben
	a sandy road ['sændɪ 'rəʊd]	eine sandige Straße / Sandstraße
	disturb somebody [dɪ'stɜ:b]	jem. stören
	Australia's Aboriginal people [æbə'rɪdʒənl]	Australiens Ureinwohner
	murder somebody ['mɜ:də]	jem. ermorden/umbringen
	settler ['setlə]	Siedler(in)

	diseases such as smallpox and tuberculosis [dɪ'zi:zɪz . . . tju:bɜ:kjʊ'ləʊsɪs]	Krankheiten wie Pocken und Tuberkulose
	survive (something) [sə'vaɪv]	(etw.) überleben
	religion [rɪ'lɪdʒən]	Religion
	their purpose in life ['pɜ:pəs]	ihr ("Zweck im Leben") Lebensinhalt
	ill health [ɪl 'helθ]	schlechte Gesundheit
	their ancient culture ['eɪnʃənt 'kʌltʃə]	ihre alte Kultur
6C	meaningful sentences ['sentənsɪz]	sinnvolle Sätze; Sätze, die einen Sinn haben
	invite somebody [ɪn'vaɪt]	jem. einladen
	founder ['faʊndə]	Gründer(in)
	bury somebody ['berɪ]	jem. begraben
	seldom ['seldəm]	selten
	the distant cattle stations ['dɪstənt]	die fernen Rinderfarmen
	diagnose a disease ['daɪəgnəʊz]	eine Krankheit diagnostizieren
6D	project ['prɒdʒekt]	Projekt
	read a text out to somebody	jem. einen Text vorlesen
	keep something a secret ['si:krət]	*(secret = Geheimnis)* etw. geheimhalten

Unit 7

7A	examine [ɪg'zæmɪn]	(über)prüfen; durchsehen; genau ansehen
	reaction (to something) [rɪ'ækʃn]	Reaktion (auf etw.)
	shocked [ʃɒkt]	schockiert; empört; bestürzt
	pleased [pli:zd]	erfreut
	make up (a story) ['meɪk ʌp]	(eine Geschichte) erfinden
	spot a mistake [spɒt]	einen Fehler finden/entdecken

Neue Wörter in den Zeitungsüberschriften, S. 38 (alphabetisch)

arrest somebody [ə'rest]	jem. festnehmen/verhaften
artificial [ɑ:tɪ'fɪʃl]	künstlich; Kunst-
blind [blaɪnd]	blind *(the blind = die Blinden)*
calf [kɑ:f] – calves [kɑ:vz]	Kalb – Kälber
(the English) Channel ['tʃænl]	(der Ärmel-)Kanal
charge that prisoners were blinded ['prɪznəz]	den Vorwurf erheben, daß Häftlinge geblendet wurden
composition [kɒmpə'zɪʃn]	Komposition
ex- [eks]	ehemalig; Ex-
man-made ['mæn-meɪd]	("von Menschen gemacht") künstlich; Kunst-
notebook ['nəʊtbʊk]	Notizbuch
postal worker ['pəʊstl wɜ:kə]	Postarbeiter(in)
profit ['prɒfɪt]	Gewinn; Profit
record ['rekɔ:d]	Rekord
row [rəʊ]	rudern
skin [skɪn]	Haut
sun-powered airplane ['sʌn-paʊəd 'eəpleɪn]	Sonnenkraftflugzeug
suspect ['sʌspekt]	Verdächtige(r)
will something to someone	jem. etw. (testamentarisch) vermachen

7B	dilemma [dɪ'lemə]	Dilemma
	nuclear ['nju:klɪə]	nuklear; Kern(waffen)-; Atom(waffen)-
	not all that terrible ['terəbl]	nicht ganz so schrecklich
	article ['ɑ:tɪkl]	Artikel
	the Post Office ['pəʊst ɒfɪs]	die Post (als staatl. Einrichtung)
	a nuclear attack ['nju:klɪər ə'tæk]	ein nuklearer Angriff / Kernwaffenangriff
	struggle through the rubble ['strʌgl]	sich durch den Schutt durchkämpfen/-quälen
	radiation [reɪdɪ'eɪʃn]	(radioaktive) Strahlung
	letter box ['letə bɒks]	Briefkasten
	mail-order catalogue ['meɪl-ɔ:də kætəlɒg]	Versandhauskatalog
	district ['dɪstrɪkt]	Bezirk; (Stadt-)Viertel
	shelter ['ʃeltə]	Schutz; Zuflucht; (Luftschutz-)Keller/Bunker
	cellar ['selə]	Keller
	bunker ['bʌŋkə]	Bunker
	medical supplies ['medɪkl səplaɪz]	("medizinische Vorräte") Arzneimittel; medizinischer Bedarf
	there won't be any addresses left [ə'dresɪz]	es werden keine Adressen mehr übrig sein
	destroy something [dɪ'strɔɪ]	etw. zerstören
	the lot [lɒt]	alle(s)
	fool [fu:l]	Dummkopf; Narr; Idiot
	think something up [θɪŋk 'ʌp]	sich etw. ausdenken
	nonsense ['nɒnsəns]	Unsinn; Blödsinn; Quatsch
	produce something [prə'dju:s]	etw. produzieren/herstellen/erstellen
	a thick book [θɪk]	ein dickes Buch
	the postal service will continue [kən'tɪnju:]	der Postdienst wird weitergehen
	when the mushroom cloud has cleared ['mʌʃrʊm klaʊd]	wenn ("die Pilzwolke") der Atompilz sich verzogen hat
	humour ['hju:mə]	Humor
	it's downright criminal ['krɪmɪnl]	das ist ausgesprochen kriminell/verbrecherisch
	it might lead people to believe [bɪ'li:v]	es könnte die Leute ("führen") dazu bringen zu glauben
	fight a war ['faɪt ə 'wɔ:]	einen Krieg ("kämpfen") führen
	politician [pɒlɪ'tɪʃn]	Politiker(in)
	do damage to somebody ['dæmɪdʒ]	jem. Schaden zufügen
	enemy ['enəmɪ]	Feind
	nuclear deterrence ['nju:klɪə dɪ'terəns]	nukleare Abschreckung
	in the long run [rʌn]	auf die Dauer
	the nuclear balance ['bæləns]	das nukleare Gleichgewicht
	the superpowers ['su:pəpaʊəz]	die Supermächte
	peace [pi:s]	Frieden
	the nuclear stockpiles ['stɒkpaɪlz]	die Kernwaffenbestände/-arsenale
	nation ['neɪʃn]	Nation; Volk; Staat
	nuclear weapons ['nju:klɪə 'wepənz]	Kernwaffen
	a regional war ['ri:dʒnəl]	ein regionaler/begrenzter Krieg
	push the button ['pʊʃ ðə 'bʌtn]	(auf) den Knopf drücken
	a nuclear holocaust ['hɒləkɔ:st]	ein Atominferno
	a ban on nuclear weapons [bæn]	ein Kernwaffenverbot
	agreement [ə'gri:mənt]	Abkommen; Vertrag
	bring something about [brɪŋ ə'baʊt]	etw. zustande bringen
	a minimum of trust ['mɪnɪməm]	ein Minimum an Vertrauen
	nuclear power plant [plɑ:nt]	Kernkraftwerk
	explosion [ɪk'spləʊʒn]	Explosion

	ability [ə'bɪlətɪ]	Fähigkeit
	solve a problem [sɒlv]	ein Problem lösen
	manage to do something ['mænɪdʒ]	es schaffen, etw. zu tun
	burn [bɜ:n] – burnt [bɜ:nt] – burnt	brennen – brannte – gebrannt
	emergency exit [ɪ'mɜ:dʒənsɪ eksɪt]	Notausgang
	scientist ['saɪəntɪst]	(Natur-)Wissenschaftler(in)
	atomic energy [ə'tɒmɪk 'enədʒɪ]	Atomenergie
	coal [kəʊl]	Kohle
	a book on the history of Australia ['hɪstrɪ]	ein Buch über die Geschichte Australiens
7C	out of work [aʊt əv 'wɜ:k]	arbeitslos
	an independent nation [ɪndɪ'pendənt 'neɪʃn]	ein unabhängiger Staat
	defeat the enemy [dɪ'fi:t ðɪ 'enəmɪ]	den Feind besiegen/schlagen
	take the lead [li:d]	die Führung übernehmen
	regain [rɪ'geɪn]	wiedergewinnen/-erlangen
	the situation has improved [ɪm'pru:vd]	die Situation hat sich gebessert
	the unemployed [ʌnɪm'plɔɪd]	die Arbeitslosen
	a major strike ['meɪdʒə 'straɪk]	ein größerer Streik
	interest rate ['ɪntrəst reɪt]	Zinssatz
	international relations [rɪ'leɪʃnz]	die internationalen Beziehungen
	air/water pollution [pə'lu:ʃn]	die Luft-/Wasserverschmutzung
7D	make a point [pɔɪnt]	ein Argument vorbringen
	react to something [rɪ'ækt]	auf etw. reagieren

Unit 8

8A	secondary school ['sekəndrɪ sku:l]	Sekundarschule (= Hauptschule, Realschule od. Gymnasium)
	college ['kɒlɪdʒ]	(etwa:) Akademie, Fach(hoch)schule, Hochschule
	improve something [ɪm'pru:v]	etw. verbessern
	interpret [ɪn'tɜ:prɪt]	dolmetschen
	grammar ['græmə]	Grammatik; Sprachlehre
	an intensive course [ɪn'tensɪv]	ein Intensivkurs(us)
8B	professor [prə'fesə]	Professor(in)
	the ability . . . declines with age [dɪ'klaɪnz]	die Fähigkeit . . . nimmt mit dem Alter ab
	the well-known psychologist [saɪ'kɒlədʒɪst]	der bekannte Psychologe
	brain [breɪn]	Gehirn
	function normally ['fʌŋkʃn 'nɔ:məlɪ]	normal funktionieren/arbeiten
	provided it is kept in practice [prə'vaɪdɪd]	vorausgesetzt, es wird in Übung gehalten
	stay active ['æktɪv]	aktiv bleiben
	you need not worry ['wʌrɪ]	Sie brauchen sich keine Sorgen zu machen
	aged 60 or more [eɪdʒd]	im Alter von 60 oder mehr Jahren
	a musical instrument ['mju:zɪkl 'ɪnstrʊmənt]	ein Musikinstrument
	tests had shown [ʃəʊn]	Tests/Untersuchungen hätten gezeigt/ergeben
	elderly citizens ['eldəlɪ 'sɪtɪznz]	ältere Bürger
	achieve the same rate of progress ['prəʊgres]	die gleichen Fortschritte erzielen
	keep your mind active ['æktɪv]	("halte deinen Geist/Verstand aktiv")
	circular (letter) ['sɜ:kjʊlə]	Rundschreiben; Werbebrief
	speak English fluently / fluent English	fließend Englisch sprechen
	however well you were taught [tɔ:t]	wie gut Sie auch (immer) unterrichtet wurden
	achieve real fluency ['flu:ənsɪ]	wirkliche Geläufigkeit erreichen

	given some knowledge of English to begin with ['nɒlɪdʒ]	(etwa:) sind erst (ein)mal englische Grundkenntnisse vorhanden
	we have the know-how ['nəʊhaʊ]	wir haben die (nötige) Sachkenntnis
	from overseas [əʊvə'si:z]	aus dem Ausland; aus Europa
	pupil ['pju:pl]	Schüler(in)
	feature ['fi:tʃə]	Merkmal; Eigenschaft
	foreigner ['fɒrənə]	Ausländer(in)
	at 11 different levels ['levlz]	auf 11 verschiedenen Niveaus/Stufen
	elementary level [elɪ'mentərɪ]	Grundstufe
	advanced [əd'vɑ:nst]	fortgeschritten
	technical English ['teknɪkl]	technisches Englisch
	entrance test ['entrəns]	Eingangs-/Aufnahmetest/-prüfung
	place someone in the right class [klɑ:s]	jem. im richtigen Kurs plazieren/einstufen
	experienced teachers [ɪk'spɪərɪənst]	erfahrene Lehrer
	support somebody [sə'pɔ:t]	jem. unterstützen
	the very latest equipment [ɪ'kwɪpmənt]	die allerneueste Ausrüstung
	audio ['ɔ:dɪəʊ]	Audio-; auditiv (d. h. auf Hören bezogen: Cassette, Schallplatte, Sprachlabor etc.)
	visual ['vɪʒʊəl]	visuell (d. h. auf Sehen bezogen: Bilder, Folien, Video etc.)
	enclose something [ɪn'kləʊz]	etw. (einem Brief) beifügen/beilegen
	welcome somebody ['welkəm]	jem. begrüßen / willkommen heißen
	or indeed the whole family [ɪn'di:d]	oder gar die ganze Familie
	principal ['prɪnsəpl]	Direktor(in) (einer Schule)
	receive a letter [rɪ'si:v]	einen Brief erhalten/empfangen
	arguments in favour of the school ['feɪvə]	Argumente, die für die Schule sprechen
8C	it shouldn't be too difficult ['ʃʊdnt]	es dürfte nicht (all)zu schwierig sein
	poem ['pəʊɪm]	Gedicht
8D	intermediate level [ɪntə'mi:djət]	Mittelstufe
	general English ['dʒenrəl]	allgemeines Englisch
	intend to do something [ɪn'tend]	beabsichtigen, etw. zu tun
	I must brush up my English ['brʌʃ ʌp]	ich muß mein Englisch auffrischen
	uses of English ['ju:sɪz]	Verwendungsmöglichkeiten des Englischen
	event [ɪ'vent]	Ereignis
	general education [edjʊ'keɪʃn]	Allgemeinbildung
	convince somebody [kən'vɪns]	jem. überzeugen

Unit 9

9A	polish shoes ['pɒlɪʃ 'ʃu:z]	Schuhe polieren/putzen
	motorcycle ['məʊtəsaɪkl]	Motorrad
	hole [həʊl]	Loch
	fill a tooth [tu:θ]	einen Zahn plombieren
	since they will be staying at the same place for four weeks	da sie vier Wochen am selben Ort bleiben werden
	redecorate the sitting room [ri:'dekəreɪt]	das Wohnzimmer renovieren
	paint the garden fence ['gɑ:dn 'fens]	den Gartenzaun streichen
	mend something [mend]	etw. ausbessern/flicken/reparieren
	these trousers must be let out ['traʊzəz]	diese Hose muß weiter gemacht werden
	alter a dress ['ɔ:ltər ə 'dres]	ein Kleid ändern
	vaccinate ['væksɪneɪt]	impfen

	you must have/get your passport renewed	Sie müssen Ihren Paß verlängern lassen
9B	old folk ['əʊld fəʊk]	alte Leute
	live in fear of somebody [fɪə]	in (ständiger) Angst vor jem. leben
	youths [ju:ðz]	Jugendliche
	smash windows [smæʃ]	Fenster einschlagen
	pull up bushes ['pʊl ʌp 'bʊʃɪz]	Sträucher/Büsche (he)rausreißen
	break [breɪk]	(zer)brechen; (Fenster:) einschlagen
	several months ago [mʌnθs]	vor einigen Monaten
	a wooden fence ['wʊdn]	ein hölzerner Zaun / Holzzaun
	pull down a fence [pʊl]	einen Zaun runterreißen/abreißen
	steal washing off the line [sti:l]	Wäsche von der Leine stehlen
	she dare not go out [deə]	sie wagt nicht hinauszugehen/rauszugehen
	for fear of [fə 'fɪər əv]	aus Angst/Furcht vor
	swear [sweə]	fluchen
	street light ['stri:t laɪt]	Straßenlaterne
	occasion [ə'keɪʒn]	Gelegenheit; Anlaß
	not long ago [ə'gəʊ]	vor nicht (all)zu langer Zeit
	hit [hɪt] – hit [hɪt] – hit	treffen – traf – getroffen
	she was knocked unconscious ['nɒkt ʌn'kɒnʃəs]	sie wurde bewußtlos (geschlagen)
	council ['kaʊnsl]	(Stadt-/Gemeinde-)Rat
	protest [prə'test]	protestieren
	insufficient protection [ɪnsə'fɪʃnt]	ungenügender/unzulänglicher Schutz
	a police spokesman ['spəʊksmən]	ein Polizeisprecher
	(police) patrol [pə'trəʊl]	(Polizei-)Streife
	trouble spot ['trʌbl spɒt]	Unruheherd
	pick up the phone ['pɪk ʌp ðə 'fəʊn]	zum ("Telefon") Hörer greifen
	the youngsters ['jʌŋstəz]	die Jugendlichen/Jungen
	playground ['pleɪgraʊnd]	Spielplatz
	acceptable [ək'septəbl]	annehmbar; akzeptabel
	bungalow ['bʌŋgələʊ]	Bungalow
	we're not keen to have a playground [ki:n]	wir sind nicht scharf/erpicht darauf, einen Spielplatz zu haben
	right up to my fence [fens]	"direkt bis ran an meinen Zaun"
	it depends on how you look at it [dɪ'pendz]	es hängt davon ab / kommt ganz darauf an, wie man es sieht
	deserve to get something [dɪ'zɜ:v]	es verdienen, etw. zu bekommen
	where they can play in safety ['seɪftɪ]	wo sie in Sicherheit spielen können
	kick the ball [bɔ:l]	den Ball treten/kicken
	tile [taɪl]	(Dach-)Ziegel
	roof [ru:f]	Dach
	greenhouse ['gri:nhaʊs]	Gewächshaus
	I'd (= I would) hate that ['aɪd 'heɪt]	("ich würde das hassen") das wäre mir gar nicht recht
	nowhere ['nəʊweə]	nirgendwo(hin); nirgends
	besides [bɪ'saɪdz]	außerdem
	a piece of wasteland ['weɪstlænd]	ein Stück Ödland
	rubbish dump ['rʌbɪʃ dʌmp]	Müllkippe
	fair enough ['feər ɪ'nʌf]	in Ordnung; annehmbar; akzeptabel
	plant trees [plɑ:nt]	Bäume pflanzen
	the actual play area ['æktʃʊəl]	der eigentliche Spielbereich
	suggestion [sə'dʒestʃn]	Vorschlag; Anregung
	the playing equipment [ɪ'kwɪpmənt]	das Spielgerät

	generous ['dʒenərəs]	großzügig
9C	tooth [tu:θ] – teeth [ti:θ]	Zahn – Zähne
	advise somebody to do something [əd'vaɪz]	jem. raten, etw. zu tun
9D	supply suitable verb forms ['su:təbl]	("liefern Sie . . .") setzen Sie passende Verbformen ein
	pool [pu:l]	(Am. Billardspiel m. 15 Kugeln auf einem Tisch m. 6 Löchern)
	guard [gɑ:d]	(BE Eisenbahn:) Schaffner(in), Zugbegleiter(in)
	British Rail ['brɪtɪʃ 'reɪl]	(staatl. brit. Eisenbahngesellschaft)
	terrorize somebody ['terəraɪz]	jem. terrorisieren
	hang around the streets ['hæŋ əraʊnd]	in den Straßen herumlungern
	new housing estate ['haʊzɪŋ ɪsteɪt]	Neubausiedlung; neue Wohnsiedlung
	brewery ['brʊərɪ]	Brauerei
	the residents ['rezɪdənts]	die Bewohner/Anwohner
	argue in favour of something ['ɑ:gju: . . . 'feɪvə]	für etw. argumentieren/Gründe anführen/plädieren
	jukebox ['dʒu:kbɒks]	Musikbox; Musikautomat

Unit 10

10A	he's better off now ['betər 'ɒf]	er ist jetzt (finanziell) besser dran/gestellt
	avoid a war [ə'vɔɪd ə 'wɔ:]	einen Krieg vermeiden
	a powerful country ['paʊəfʊl]	ein mächtiges Land
	healthy ['helθɪ]	gesund
	religious [rɪ'lɪdʒəs]	religiös; gläubig; fromm
	spare time ['speə 'taɪm]	Freizeit
	democracy [dɪ'mɒkrəsɪ]	Demokratie
10B	predict what lies ahead [prɪ'dɪkt]	vorhersagen/voraussagen, was vor uns liegt
	journal ['dʒɜ:nl]	Zeitschrift
	prediction [prɪ'dɪkʃn]	Vorhersage; Voraussage; Prophezeiung
	the ordinary "horseless carriage" ['kærɪdʒ]	die gewöhnliche "pferdelose Kutsche"
	at present [ət 'preznt]	zur Zeit; im Augenblick/Moment; derzeit
	the wealthy ['welθɪ]	die Wohlhabenden/Reichen
	come into common use ['kɒmən 'ju:s]	in allgemeinen Gebrauch kommen
	set foot on the moon [fʊt . . . mu:n]	den Mond betreten
	a scientific journal [saɪən'tɪfɪk]	eine (natur)wissenschaftliche Zeitschrift
	land on the moon [mu:n]	auf dem Mond landen
	human beings ['hju:mən 'bi:ɪŋz]	("menschliche Wesen") Menschen
	a Greek poet ['gri:k 'pəʊɪt]	ein griechischer Dichter
	century ['sentʃərɪ]	Jahrhundert
	in spite of this advice [əd'vaɪs]	trotz dieses Rat(e)s
	find ready ears [ɪəz]	("bereite") offene Ohren finden
	a journalist named Croly ['krəʊlɪ]	ein Journalist namens Croly
	publish a book ['pʌblɪʃ]	ein Buch veröffentlichen/herausbringen/verlegen
	title ['taɪtl]	Titel
	glimpses of the future ['glɪmsɪz]	"(Ein-)Blicke in die Zukunft"
	author ['ɔ:θə]	Autor(in); Verfasser(in)
	judge something [dʒʌdʒ]	etw. beurteilen; ein Urteil üb. etw. fällen
	control the business world [kən'trəʊl]	die Geschäftswelt kontrollieren/beherrschen
	motion picture ['məʊʃn 'pɪktʃə]	Film
	aeroplane ['eərəpleɪn]	(BE) Flugzeug
	electricity [ɪlek'trɪsətɪ]	Elektrizität; (elektr.) Strom

	(power) source [sɔːs]	(Energie-)Quelle
	indeed [ɪnˈdiːd]	in der Tat; tatsächlich; wirklich
	striking cases [ˈstraɪkɪŋ ˈkeɪsɪz]	auffallende/bemerkenswerte/eindrucksvolle Fälle
	countless others [ˈkaʊntləs ˈʌðəz]	zahllose/unzählige andere
	the truth [truːθ]	die Wahrheit
	repeat something [rɪˈpiːt]	etw. wiederholen
	futurology [fjuːtʃəˈrɒlədʒɪ]	Futurologie
	established as a science [ɪˈstæblɪʃt]	als Wissenschaft etabliert
	forecast future developments [ˈfɔːkɑːst]	(zu)künftige Entwicklungen vorher-/voraussagen
	trend [trend]	Trend; Tendenz
	society [səˈsaɪətɪ]	(die) Gesellschaft
	futurologist [fjuːtʃəˈrɒlədʒɪst]	Futurologe/Futurologin
	statistics [stəˈtɪstɪks]	Statistiken
	crystal ball [ˈkrɪstl ˈbɔːl]	Kristallkugel (der Hellseherin)
	comment [ˈkɒment]	Kommentar; Stellungnahme
	taxpayer [ˈtækspeɪə]	Steuerzahler(in)
	the Bible [ˈbaɪbl]	die Bibel
	each day has troubles of its own [ˈtrʌblz]	jeder Tag hat seine eigenen Sorgen
	enable someone to do something [ɪˈneɪbl]	jem. befähigen, etw. zu tun
	beat [biːt] – beat [biːt] – beaten [ˈbiːtn]	schlagen – schlug – geschlagen
	(e.g. world) champion [ˈtʃæmpjən]	(z. B. Welt-)Meister
	an original scientific discovery [əˈrɪdʒənl]	eine originelle wissenschaftliche Entdeckung
	worthy of a Nobel Prize [ˈwɜːðɪ . . . nəʊˈbel ˈpraɪz]	eines Nobelpreises würdig
	own something [əʊn]	etw. besitzen
	car pool [ˈkɑː puːl]	Fahrgemeinschaft
	moped [ˈməʊped]	Moped; Mofa
	blackmail somebody [ˈblækmeɪl]	jem. erpressen
	terrorist [ˈterərɪst]	Terrorist(in)
	a nuclear device [ˈnjuːklɪə dɪˈvaɪs]	ein atomarer Sprengkörper
	a portable telephone [ˈpɔːtəbl]	ein tragbares Telefon
	mini- [ˈmɪnɪ]	Mini-
	thaw [θɔː]	(auf)tauen
	they're unable to read [ʌnˈeɪbl]	sie ("sind unfähig zu") können nicht lesen
	electric vehicle [ɪˈlektrɪk ˈvɪəkl]	Elektrofahrzeug
	come into widespread use [ˈwaɪdspred ˈjuːs]	in ("weitverbreiteten") allgemeinen Gebrauch kommen
	in the early stages [ˈsteɪdʒɪz]	in den frühen Stadien
	cancer can be cured [ˈkænsə . . . ˈkjʊəd]	Krebs kann geheilt werden
	in the tropics [ˈtrɒpɪks]	in den Tropen
	is painfully aware [ˈpeɪnfʊlɪ əˈweə]	ist sich schmerzlich bewußt
	ice age [ˈaɪs eɪdʒ]	Eiszeit
	gas [gæs]	Gas
	which are likely to come true? [truː]	welche werden sich ("wahrscheinlich") wohl bewahrheiten?
	the year is past [pɑːst]	das Jahr ist vorüber/vergangen
10C	breathe [briːð]	atmen
	sound [saʊnd]	Klang; Sound
	guitar [gɪˈtɑː]	Gitarre
	turn something/someone down [tɜːn]	etw./jem. ablehnen/zurückweisen
	get hold of something [get ˈhəʊld]	etw. in die Hände bekommen
10D	boot [buːt]	Stiefel
	stamp on something [stæmp]	auf etw. stampfen/trampeln

	novel ['nɒvl]	Roman
	a totalitarian police state [təʊtælɪ'teərɪən]	ein totalitärer Polizeistaat
	rule a country [ru:l]	ein Land beherrschen/regieren

Unit 11

1A	grand puzzle ['grænd 'pʌzl]	großes Rätsel
	tobacco [tə'bækəʊ]	Tabak
	pipe [paɪp]	(Tabaks-)Pfeife
	you can't wash properly ['prɒpəlɪ]	man kann (sich) nicht richtig waschen
	gallon ['gælən]	(BE = 4,546 l; AE = 3,78 l)
	litre ['li:tə]	Liter
	Trades Union Congress ['kɒŋgres]	(Dachverband der brit. Gewerkschaften)
	cent [sent]	(= $^{1}/_{100}$ Dollar)
	calculator ['kælkjʊleɪtə]	Rechner
	boxing match ['bɒksɪŋ mætʃ]	Boxkampf
	The Singing Fool ['sɪŋɪŋ 'fu:l]	(einer der ersten Tonfilme, USA 1928, m. Al Jolson)
	whom many called . . . [hu:m]	den viele . . . nannten
	Alice('s Adventures) in Wonderland ['ælɪsɪz]	(Märchen von Lewis Carroll, 1865)
	fortunately ['fɔ:tʃnətlɪ]	glücklicherweise
	murder ['mɜ:də]	Mord
	the two are not alike [ə'laɪk]	die beiden sind nicht gleich
	Hamlet ['hæmlɪt]	(Trauerspiel von Shakespeare, 1601)
	the border between the two countries ['bɔ:də]	die Grenze zwischen den beiden Ländern
	send a letter by airmail ['eəmeɪl]	einen Brief per/mit Luftpost schicken
	rose [rəʊz]	Rose
	baggage ['bægɪdʒ]	(AE u. Luftreisen:) Gepäck
	cow [kaʊ]	Kuh
	republic [rɪ'pʌblɪk]	Republik
	ball pen ['bɔ:l pen]	Kugelschreiber
1B	he's got his leg in plaster ['plɑ:stə]	er hat das Bein in Gips
	dash downstairs ['dæʃ daʊn'steəz]	die Treppe runter stürmen/sausen
	miss a step ['mɪs ə 'step]	eine Stufe verfehlen
	slip [slɪp]	ausrutschen; ausgleiten
	he could have broken his neck ['brəʊkən]	er hätte sich den Hals / das Genick brechen können
	bruise [bru:z]	blauer Fleck; Bluterguß
	incidentally [ɪnsɪ'dentəlɪ]	übrigens
	an electronic miracle [ɪlek'trɒnɪk 'mɪrəkl]	ein elektronisches Wunder
	a toy [tɔɪ]	ein Spielzeug
	a packet of typing paper ['pækɪt]	ein Paket / eine Packung Schreibmaschinenpapier
	the built-in calculator ['bɪlt-ɪn]	der eingebaute Rechner
	kilogram ['kɪləgræm]	Kilo(gramm)
	memory ['memərɪ]	Gedächtnis
	display [dɪ'spleɪ]	Display (= anzeigende Funktionseinheit im elektronischen System)
	one-third [wʌn-'θɜ:d]	ein Drittel
	e.g. (= for example) [fər ɪg'zɑ:mpl]	z. B. (= zum Beispiel)
	square brackets ['skweə 'brækɪts]	eckige Klammern
	the tiny thing ['taɪnɪ]	das winzige Ding
	battery ['bætərɪ]	Batterie

	silent ['saɪlənt]	ruhig; lautlos
	impress somebody [ɪm'pres]	jem. beeindrucken
	wristwatch ['rɪstwɒtʃ]	Armbanduhr
	you wonder what will come next ['wʌndə]	man fragt sich / möchte wissen, was als nächstes kommt
	what does the print look like? [prɪnt]	wie sieht der Druck aus?
11C	travel agent ['trævl eɪdʒənt]	Reisebüro
	crazy ['kreɪzɪ]	verrückt; wahnsinnig
	grandmaster [grænd'mɑːstə]	(Schach:) Großmeister
	the car park closes at 7 p.m. ['kləʊzɪz]	das Parkhaus macht um 19 Uhr zu
11D	go into politics ['pɒlətɪks]	in die Politik gehen
	it's over ['əʊvə]	es ist vorbei/vorüber
	IQ (= intelligence quotient) ['aɪ'kjuː]	Intelligenzquotient
	alibi ['ælɪbaɪ]	Alibi
	weight [weɪt]	Gewicht
	it's a good make [meɪk]	es ist eine gute Marke / ein gutes Fabrikat
	comment on something ['kɒment]	sich zu etw. äußern
	slogan ['sləʊgən]	Slogan; Motto; Wahlspruch; Parole
	wish someone a speedy recovery [rɪ'kʌvərɪ]	jem. ("eine schnelle Genesung") gute Besserung wünschen
	Walkman ['wɔːkmən]	(kleiner, tragbarer Cassettenrecorder, ohne Lautsprecher, nur mit Kopfhörer)

Unit 12

12A	eating/drinking habits ['hæbɪts]	Eß-/Trinkgewohnheiten
	supper ['sʌpə]	Abendessen; Abendbrot
	oyster ['ɔɪstə]	Auster
	chew tobacco ['tʃuː tə'bækəʊ]	Tabak kauen
	we bake our own bread [bred]	wir backen unser Brot selbst
	health-food fan ['helθ-fuːd fæn]	Reformkost-Fan(atiker[in])
	vegetarian [vedʒɪ'teərɪən]	Vegetarier(in); vegetarisch
	slim [slɪm]	schlank
	calories ['kælərɪz]	Kalorien
	unsprayed fruit ['ʌnspreɪd 'fruːt]	ungespritztes Obst
12B	taste [teɪst]	Geschmack
	keep up with demand [dɪ'mɑːnd]	mit der Nachfrage Schritt halten
	pure [pjʊə]	rein
	convenience foods are giving way to health foods	Fertigkost macht Reformkost Platz
	wet fish ['wet fɪʃ]	("nasser Fisch") Frischfisch
	they're the order of the day ['ɔːdə]	sie sind an der Tagesordnung
	bran [bræn]	Kleie
	wholemeal ['həʊlmiːl]	Vollkorn(-)
	brown rice ['braʊn 'raɪs]	("brauner") ungeschälter Reis
	for enjoyment [ɪn'dʒɔɪmənt]	zum Vergnügen/Spaß
	a trend towards brown bread [tə'wɔːdz]	ein Trend (hin) zu Graubrot/Roggenbrot
	switch to something [swɪtʃ]	sich auf etw. umstellen
	free-range eggs [friː-'reɪnʒ egz]	Eier von freilaufenden Hühnern
	appetizing ['æpɪtaɪzɪŋ]	appetitanregend; verlockend; appetitlich
	battery production ['bætərɪ prədʌkʃn]	Intensiverzeugung
	pork [pɔːk]	Schweinefleisch

lamb [læm]	Lamm(fleisch)
consume [kən'sju:m]	verzehren; konsumieren
boom [bu:m]	Boom; Hochkonjunktur
in portions ['pɔ:ʃnz]	in Portionen/Teilen
that's due to the price advantage [dju:]	das ist auf den Preisvorteil zurückzuführen
fibre ['faɪbə]	Faser
the Frenchman Balzac ['bælzæk]	der Franzose Balzac
an extraordinary eater [ɪk'strɔ:dnrɪ]	ein außergewöhnlicher Esser
cutlet ['kʌtlɪt]	Kotelett; Schnitzel
duck [dʌk]	Ente
partridge ['pɑ:trɪdʒ]	Rebhuhn
dessert [dɪ'zɜ:t]	Nachtisch; Dessert
Lord [lɔ:d]	(hoher engl. Adelstitel)
soda water ['səʊdə wɔ:tə]	Sodawasser
flour ['flaʊə]	Mehl
sugar ['ʃʊgə]	Zucker
muffin ['mʌfɪn]	(eine Art Semmel/Brötchen)
frugal ['fru:gl]	einfach; sparsam; genügsam
stone [stəʊn]	(1 stone = 14 pounds = 6.348 kilograms)
philosopher [fɪ'lɒsəfə]	Philosoph(in)
she remarked to him [rɪ'mɑ:kt]	sie bemerkte/äußerte ihm gegenüber
poison ['pɔɪzn]	Gift
reply [rɪ'plaɪ]	antworten; erwidern
for I've been drinking it for 65 years	denn ich trinke es schon seit 65 Jahren
I'm not dead yet [ded]	ich bin (immer) noch nicht tot
2C that applies to him too [ə'plaɪz]	das gilt auch für ihn
2D silly questions ['sɪlɪ]	alberne/blöde/dumme/doofe Fragen
regard something as healthy [rɪ'gɑ:d]	etw. für gesund halten
wisdom ['wɪzdəm]	Weisheit; Klugheit
sauce [sɔ:s]	Soße
vegetarianism [vedʒɪ'teərɪənɪzm]	Vegetarismus; vegetarische Lebensweise
rear animals [rɪə]	Tiere großziehen/aufziehen
inhumane(ly) [ɪnhju:'meɪn]	inhuman; grausam
cruel [krʊəl]	grausam
restless ['restləs]	unruhig; rastlos
on average ['ævrɪdʒ]	im Durchschnitt; durchschnittlich
stuffed with chemicals ['stʌft . . . 'kemɪklz]	mit Chemikalien vollgestopft
destroy an animal [dɪ'strɔɪ]	ein Tier töten/einschläfern
non- [nɒn]	nicht-; un-
in Europe at any rate ['jʊərəp]	in Europa jedenfalls
heavy work ['hevɪ]	schwere Arbeit; Schwerarbeit
animals and us ['ænɪməlz]	die Tiere und wir
hens lay eggs [leɪ]	Hennen legen Eier
cage [keɪdʒ]	Käfig
force somebody to do something [fɔ:s]	jem. zwingen, etw. zu tun
beyond doubt [bɪ'jɒnd 'daʊt]	ohne Zweifel
they would picture the Devil in human form ['devl]	sie würden sich den Teufel in menschlicher Form vorstellen

Unit 13

13A	jumble something ['dʒʌmbl]	etw. durcheinanderbringen/-werfen
	personality [pɜ:sə'nælətɪ]	Persönlichkeit
	the circled letters ['sɜ:kld]	die "eingekreisten"/"umkringelten" Buchstaben
	it's relevant to the topic of this Unit ['reləvənt]	es ist für das Thema dieser Lektion relevant
13B	handgun ['hændgʌn]	Handfeuerwaffe
	ban something [bæn]	etw. verbieten
	pass a law ['pɑ:s ə 'lɔ:]	ein Gesetz verabschieden
	mayor [meə]	Bürgermeister(in)
	her predecessor ['pri:dɪsesə]	ihr(e) Vorgänger(in)
	supervisor ['su:pəvaɪzə]	(in manchen amerik. Stadtverwaltungen, etwa:) Dezernent(in); Senator(in)
	shoot [ʃu:t] – shot [ʃɒt] – shot	erschießen – erschoß – erschossen
	city hall [sɪtɪ 'hɔ:l]	Rathaus
	a drive for stronger gun control ['strɒŋgə 'gʌn kəntrəʊl]	eine Aktion/Initiative für strengere Schußwaffenkontrolle
	handguns were involved [ɪn'vɒlvd]	Handfeuerwaffen spielten eine Rolle / waren beteiligt
	were commonly used ['kɒmənlɪ]	wurden häufig benutzt
	robberies and rapes ['rɒbərɪz]	Raubüberfälle und Vergewaltigungen
	the illegal possession of handguns [pə'zeʃn]	der illegale Besitz von Handfeuerwaffen
	punish something ['pʌnɪʃ]	etw. bestrafen
	National Rifle Association [əsəʊsɪ'eɪʃn]	"Nationaler Schützenverband" *(rifle = Gewehr)*
	defend something strongly [dɪ'fend]	etw. energisch verteidigen
	the right to own firearms ['faɪərɑ:mz]	das Recht, Feuer-/Schußwaffen zu besitzen
	criminal ['krɪmɪnl]	Kriminelle(r); Verbrecher(in)
	law-abiding citizens ['lɔ:-əbaɪdɪŋ 'sɪtɪznz]	gesetzestreue/ordnungsliebende Bürger
	outlaw something ['aʊtlɔ:]	etw. für gesetzeswidrig/ungesetzlich erklären
	community [kə'mju:nətɪ]	Gemeinde; Kommune
	was required by law [rɪ'kwaɪəd]	war gesetzlich verpflichtet
	load a gun ['ləʊd ə 'gʌn]	eine Schußwaffe laden
	in (good) working order ['wɜ:kɪŋ 'ɔ:də]	betriebsbereit; schußbereit
	say amen to something ['eɪ'men]	("zu etw. Amen sagen") etw. befürworten
	the only perfect solution [sə'lu:ʃn]	die einzig(e) perfekte Lösung
	the high crime rate ['kraɪm reɪt]	die hohe Kriminalität
	where he declared [dɪ'kleəd]	wo er erklärte
	high school ['haɪ sku:l]	(in den USA: weiterführende allgemeinbildende Schule; Mittel- u. Oberschule)
	do you know how to handle a gun? ['hændl]	weißt du, wie man mit einer Schußwaffe umgeht?
	a sharp drop in burglaries ['bɜ:glərɪz]	ein starker Rückgang der Einbrüche
	brisk [brɪsk]	flott; flink; lebhaft
	sign [saɪn]	Schild
	never mind the dog [maɪnd]	achten Sie nicht auf / vergessen Sie den Hund
	beware of the owner [bɪ'weə]	nehmen Sie sich in acht vor dem Besitzer
	bear arms [beər 'ɑ:mz]	Waffen tragen
	shoot somebody [ʃu:t]	(auch:) auf jem. schießen
	accidental(ly) [æksɪ'dentl]	zufällig; versehentlich; aus Versehen
	gunshot wound [wu:nd]	Schußwunde
	estimate ['estɪmeɪt]	schätzen
	according to estimates ['estɪməts]	nach Schätzungen; Schätzungen zufolge
	the combined armed services [kəm'baɪnd]	die vereinigten Streitkräfte

	that's a matter of course [kɔ:s]	das ist eine Selbstverständlichkeit
	bodyguard ['bɒdɪgɑ:d]	Leibwächter; Leibwache
	versus ['vɜ:səs]	gegen
	compile a list [kəm'paɪl]	eine Liste zusammenstellen/erstellen
	the right . . . shall not be infringed [ɪn'frɪnʒd]	das Recht . . . soll/darf nicht verletzt werden
	the Second Amendment to the Constitution [ə'mendmənt . . . kɒnstɪ'tju:ʃn]	der Zweite Zusatz zur Verfassung
13C	wallet ['wɒlɪt]	Brieftasche
	come on, folks! [fəʊks]	na los, Leute!
	hand the money over ['mʌnɪ]	das Geld übergeben/aushändigen
	careful(ly) ['keəfʊl]	sorgfältig
	pass judgment on somebody ['dʒʌdʒmənt]	über jem. ein Urteil fällen
13D	how do they manage? ['mænɪdʒ]	wie kommen sie zurecht?
	householder ['haʊshəʊldə]	Haus-/Wohnungsinhaber(in)
	self-defence [self-dɪ'fens]	Selbstverteidigung
	adult-education centre ['ædʌlt-edjʊ'keɪʃn sentə]	("Erwachsenenbildungszentrum") (etwa:) Volkshochschule
	first aid ['fɜ:st 'eɪd]	Erste Hilfe
	birch [bɜ:tʃ]	Rute
	the death penalty ['deθ penltɪ]	die Todesstrafe
	intelligence [ɪn'telɪdʒəns]	Intelligenz
	breed [bri:d] – bred [bred] – bred	(z. B. Pflanzen) züchten – züchtete – gezüchtet
	have a vote (on something) [vəʊt]	(über etw.) abstimmen

Unit 14

14A	relative ['relətɪv]	Verwandte(r)
	how long has that been going on?	wie lange ist das schon im Gange?
	she has started her apprenticeship [ə'prentɪʃɪp]	sie hat ihre Lehre/Lehrzeit begonnen
14B	return from a trip [rɪ'tɜ:n]	von einer Reise zurückkommen/zurückkehren
	clipping ['klɪpɪŋ]	(hauptsächlich AE) Zeitungsausschnitt
	prepare somebody for something [prɪ'peə]	jem. auf etw. vorbereiten
	automobile accident ['ɔ:təməbi:l]	(AE) Autounfall
	while we were gone [gɒn]	(AE) während wir weg/verreist waren
	hit somebody [hɪt]	jem. (z. B. mit dem Auto) anfahren
	rainstorm ['reinstɔ:m]	heftiger Regenguß
	as if we've known you forever (AE) / for ever (BE) [fə'revə]	als ob wir euch schon ewig kennen
	fondly ['fɒndlɪ]	(als Briefschluß etwa:) alles Liebe
	as if you were Susanne [wɜ:]	als wenn Sie Susanne wären
	best wishes for a speedy recovery [rɪ'kʌvərɪ]	viele gute Wünsche für eine baldige Genesung
	feelings of friendship ['frendʃɪp]	("Gefühle der Freundschaft") freundschaftliche Gefühle
	lay workers off [leɪ . . . 'ɒf]	Arbeiter (besonders: vorübergehend) entlassen/freisetzen
	he's in bad shape [ʃeɪp]	er ist in schlechter Verfassung
	growing pains ['grəʊɪŋ peɪnz]	Wachstumsschmerzen
	stress [stres]	Streß; Überlastung
	ulcer ['ʌlsə]	(z. B. Magen-)Geschwür
	blood pressure ['blʌd preʃə]	Blutdruck
	sad [sæd]	traurig

	she was so well-mannered [wel-'mænəd]	sie hatte so gute Manieren / war so wohlerzogen
	cartoon movie [kɑ:'tu:n mu:vɪ]	Zeichentrickfilm
	she was very lazy ['leɪzɪ]	sie war sehr faul
	she passed her (AE) driver's / (BE) driving test	sie bestand die Fahrprüfung
	it's snowing ['snəʊɪŋ]	es schneit ("ist am Schneien")
	decorate the Christmas tree ['dekəreɪt]	den Weihnachtsbaum schmücken
	forgive me [fə'gɪv]	verzeih/vergib mir
	we appreciate your friendship [ə'pri:ʃɪeɪt . . . 'frendʃɪp]	wir wissen eure Freundschaft zu schätzen / sind dankbar für eure Freundschaft
	we sincerely hope [sɪn'sɪəlɪ]	wir hoffen aufrichtig
	a blessed Christmas ['blesɪd]	ein gesegnetes Weihnachtsfest
	the snow puts us into the mood for Christmas [mu:d]	der Schnee versetzt uns in Weihnachtsstimmung
	fairyland ['feərɪlænd]	Märchenland
	American rather than British English ['rɑ:ðə]	eher amerikanisches als britisches Englisch
	happenings ['hæpənɪŋz]	Ereignisse; Vorkommnisse
14C	we're snowed in ['snəʊd 'ɪn]	wir sind eingeschneit
14D	where did you meet? [mi:t]	wo haben Sie sich kennengelernt?
	on entering the house ['entərɪŋ]	beim Betreten des Hauses
	what a terrible mess! ['terəbl 'mes]	was für ein schreckliches Durcheinander!
	turn out the drawers [drɔ:z]	die Schubladen (aus)leeren
	break things [breɪk]	Dinge/Sachen kaputtmachen

Unit 15

15A	signpost ['saɪnpəʊst]	Wegweiser
	confusing [kən'fju:zɪŋ]	verwirrend
	no waiting/stopping/standing	Halteverbot
	weekday ['wi:kdeɪ]	Wochentag; Werktag
	meter ['mi:tə]	Parkuhr
	surgery hours ['sɜ:dʒərɪ aʊəz]	Sprechstunden (eines Arztes/Zahn-/Tierarztes)
	warning ['wɔ:nɪŋ]	Warnung
15B	dismiss somebody [dɪs'mɪs]	jem. entlassen
	swear at somebody [sweə]	gegenüber jem. Schimpfworte benutzen; jem. beschimpfen
	warehouseman ['weəhaʊsmən]	Lagerarbeiter; Lagerist
	unload [ʌn'ləʊd]	ausladen; abladen; entladen
	19 tons of carpeting [tʌnz . . . 'kɑ:pɪtɪŋ]	19 Tonnen Teppiche
	he was fed up [fed 'ʌp]	er hatte die Nase voll
	transport manager ['trænspɔ:t mænɪdʒə]	Versandleiter(in)
	floor polish ['flɔ: pɒlɪʃ]	Bohnerwachs
	he lost his temper ['tempə]	er verlor die Beherrschung/Nerven
	bugger off! ['bʌgər 'ɒf]	hau ab!; zieh Leine!
	no previous complaints against him ['pri:vjəs]	("keine vorherigen") bisher keine Klagen/Beschwerden gegen ihn
	dismissal [dɪs'mɪsl]	Entlassung
	apply to somebody [ə'plaɪ]	sich an jem. wenden
	industrial tribunal [ɪn'dʌstrɪəl traɪ'bju:nl]	(etwa:) Arbeitsgericht
	he was in a bad temper ['tempə]	er war schlechter Laune
	sack an employee ['sæk ən emplɔɪ'i:]	eine(n) Arbeitnehmer(in)/Mitarbeiter(in) rausschmeißen

	decide a case [dɪ'saɪd]	einen Fall entscheiden
	fail to do something [feɪl]	es versäumen, etw. zu tun; etw. nicht tun
	obey the lights [ə'beɪ]	"der Ampel gehorchen"
	architect ['ɑːkɪtekt]	Architekt(in)
	gradually ['grædjʊəlɪ]	allmählich; nach und nach
	junction ['dʒʌŋkʃn]	(Straßen-)Kreuzung
	when it came to her turn / was her turn [tɜːn]	als sie dran / an der Reihe war
	hesitate ['hezɪteɪt]	zögern
	courage ['kʌrɪdʒ]	Mut; Courage
	she ended up in court [kɔːt]	sie landete vor Gericht
	charged with failing to obey the lights	"angeklagt der/wegen Mißachtung der Ampel"
	out of action ['ækʃn]	außer Betrieb
	the cars in front of her [frʌnt]	die Autos vor ihr
	judge [dʒʌdʒ]	Richter(in)
	convict somebody [kən'vɪkt]	jem. verurteilen
	mongrel ['mʌŋgrəl]	Bastard; (Promenaden-)Mischung
	puppy ['pʌpɪ]	Welpe; junger Hund
	five days before [bɪ'fɔː]	fünf Tage vorher
	she decided to have Blackie put down	sie beschloß, Blackie einschläfern zu lassen
	to save him further suffering ['sʌfərɪŋ]	um ihm weitere(s) Leiden zu ersparen
	the vet's surgery ['vets 'sɜːdʒərɪ]	der Behandlungsraum / die Praxis des Tierarztes
	she recognized him at once ['rekəgnaɪzd]	sie erkannte ihn sofort
	how do you account for the fact [ə'kaʊnt]	wie erklären Sie sich die Tatsache
5C	the policeman booked her [pə'liːsmən]	der Polizist schrieb sie auf / zeigte sie an
	an apology [ə'pɒlədʒɪ]	eine Entschuldigung
	award something to somebody [ə'wɔːd]	jem. etw. zusprechen/zuerkennen
	compensation [kɒmpen'seɪʃn]	Entschädigung
	after the hearing ['hɪərɪŋ]	nach der Verhandlung
	two-and-a-half grand [grænd]	zweieinhalbtausend Pfund; zweieinhalb "Riesen"
	under the same circumstances ['sɜːkəmstənsɪz]	unter den gleichen Umständen
5D	apologize [ə'pɒlədʒaɪz]	sich entschuldigen
	detective [dɪ'tektɪv]	Kriminalbeamte(r); Detektiv

Wendungen für das Alltagsgespräch (Redeabsichten/Sprechintentionen)

(Siehe auch:
Welcome 1, S. 99 ff.
Welcome 2, S. 104 f.)

Abraten
Don't do that.
I wouldn't do that if I were you.
I wouldn't advise you to do that.
That doesn't seem a very good idea (to me).
There must be a better solution than that.

Absicht ausdrücken
I'm going to write her a letter.
That's what I'm going to do.
What are you going to do now?
What do you intend to do now?

Anbieten, etw. zu tun
Shall/May/Can I help you?
Let me help you.
Would you like me to go there for you?
How about me/my doing it for you?

Anerkennung aussprechen
Well done!
I'd like to / Let me congratulate you on a fine job.
Excellent! / Congratulations!
You've done a fine job.

Anklage formulieren
You are charged with robbery.

Antipathie, Abneigung ausdrücken
I don't like him at all.
It seems he has taken a dislike to me.
I'm not very keen on him, I must say.
He's awful.

Bedauern ausdrücken
I'm terribly sorry that happened.
I feel no regret about what I did.
It was with deep regret that I heard the news of his death.

Befehlen
Do it at once.
I want you to do it at once.
You must / are to go there at once.

Bereitschaft ausdrücken
I'm (quite) willing to help in any way I can.
I'm prepared to work hard.
I'm not willing/prepared to do that sort of thing.
I'll help.

Bestätigen
Yes indeed. He/She/It has indeed.
So he/she/it has.

Bitten
(Would you) Please do that for me.
May I ask you to do that for me.

Dank ausdrücken und darauf reagieren
Thank you very much (indeed). – Not at all. / That's all right.
Many thanks for helping me (with the bags). – You're welcome.
We appreciate your help/friendliness/friendship.
I'm very grateful for the advice you gave me.

Einladen
Would you like to join us (for a cup of tea)?
Why don't you . . .
Come round for a drink this evening.

Entrüstung ausdrücken
Just imagine . . .
How dare you (say/do such a thing)!
Honestly! / Really!

(Sich) Entschuldigen
I'm (very/terribly/extremely/deeply) sorry (for) . . .
I'd like to apologize for what I've done.
We'd like to offer our apologies (for) . . .

Enttäuschung ausdrücken
I'm not at all happy with the results.
I was disappointed to hear that you can't come.
It's all very disappointing.
It's a pity you can't come.

Folgerung ziehen
If that is so, then . . .
It follows from this that . . .
In that case we'll have to change our plans.

Freude ausdrücken
I can't tell you how glad/happy/pleased I am.
It's been a pleasure/joy meeting/seeing/helping you.
Oh, that's lovely!

Furcht ausdrücken
We dare not go out at night for fear of being robbed.
I'm afraid of you / him / her / the dog.

Gewohnheit ausdrücken
We usually go to the seaside for our summer holiday.
I'm in the habit of going for a walk after lunch.
We used to spend our holidays at the seaside when we were young.

Gleichgültigkeit ausdrücken
It's all the same to me.
I don't mind/care what you do.
That doesn't bother me.

Gruß bestellen
She sends (you) her love.
She's asked me to give you her love.
Please give my love to Betty.
Jimmy sends his regards / best wishes.
Give my regards to your mother.

Hypothetisch reden
I wouldn't do that if I were you.
I would have done it quite differently.

Kommentieren
I think / In my opinion X was right/wrong in saying . . .
X shouldn't have said/done that.
X should have / ought to have done something else.
It's right/wrong to do that sort of thing.

Meinungsübereinstimmung und -verschiedenheit ausdrücken
I agree with you/him/her (on that point).
I don't think you're right (on that point).
I strongly disagree with you there.

Mitfreude ausdrücken
Congratulations!
I'm so glad/happy you . . .
Isn't it wonderful (the way) you . . .

Möglichkeit ausdrücken
That may/might/could be the postman.
That may/might/could have been the postman.
He may/might/could be at home.
She may/might/could have been at home.
Is it / Would it be possible that . . .
That sort of thing is impossible.
That can't have been the postman.

Mutmaßen
I wonder if that was Bill.
I wonder / I'd like to know who said that.
Could that be / have been Bill?

Notwendigkeit ausdrücken
You must hurry.
You need not worry / don't need/have to worry.
There's no need for you to worry.
That really wasn't necessary.
Will it be necessary for all of us to be there?

Präferenz ausdrücken
I'd rather buy something else.
I'd prefer (to buy) something else.
This one is nicer / better / more beautiful.

Raten, Rat erbitten
I wouldn't do that if I were you.
I (would) advise you to accept the offer.
If you take my advice, you'll accept the offer.
What shall I do? What do you advise me to do?
What would you do in my position?

Reklamieren, sich beschweren
Instead of dry-cleaning them, you washed them.
The curtains should have been dry-cleaned but you washed them instead.
I'm holding you responsible for the mistake.
If you don't . . ., I'll . . .
I must insist . . .

Rückfrage stellen
Pardon? What was it you wanted to know?
What did you say happened to him/her/it?
Sorry, I didn't quite catch what you said.
Could you say that again, please?

Sorge ausdrücken
I'm (very/deeply/terribly) worried about him/her/it.
I'm afraid there might/could be . . .
What worries me is . . .

Sympathie, Neigung ausdrücken
I like him/her/it very much.
He's a very nice/pleasant boy.

Trauer ausdrücken
We're all very sad about his/her death.
You have my heartfelt/deep(est) sympathy.

Überzeugung audrücken
I'm convinced / I have no doubt that X is right.
I strongly believe / I'm quite sure that X is innocent.

Ungewißheit ausdrücken
I'm not (quite) sure that they will come.
I'm very much in doubt whether we're doing the right thing.

Veranlassen
Please arrange for the necessary bookings to be made.
See to it that it is done immediately.
Get him to do it as soon as possible.
How do I get my passport renewed?
Have some prints made of this photo.

Verbieten
You must not / mustn't play on the stairs.
I forbid you to play on the stairs.
I don't want you to play on the stairs.

Vermutung ausdrücken
I don't expect he's here.
I suspect something's wrong.
I suppose that's the best thing you can do.
My assumption is that she is his wife.

Versprechen, etwas zu tun
I promise to look after her.

(Eine Aussage) Verstärken
I do hope you'll come again.
You yourself told me she was coming.
It was you who told me she was coming.
It hurts like hell.
They made a hell of a noise. It was a hell of a job.
He was talking all the blasted time.
It was so dark I couldn't see a darn thing.

Verwunderung ausdrücken
I'm surprised to hear that.
I find it amazing the way you talk about things you know nothing about.
What a surprising / an amazing thing to say!
Oh Lord! / Good Lord!

Vorschlag machen
Why don't we go to the cinema for a change?
Let's go to the cinema (for a change), shall we?
What about going for a walk?
How about a walk in the park?

Warnen
I warn you not to go near the dog.
Beware of the dog.
I wouldn't go near the dog if I were you.
You'd better not go near the dog.

Widersprechen
Frank Sinatra's a wonderful singer, isn't he?
– Oh, d'you really think so?
– Well, I'm not very keen on him.
– He's not very good if you ask me.
– Well, personally I don't like him at all.
– No, he isn't.

Wunsch ausdrücken
I'd love to see that film.
I'd like to come here again some time.
I wish you were here.
It would be lovely if . . .

Zufriedenheit ausdrücken
I'm (quite/very) happy/satisfied with the results.
How are things? – (I) Can't complain.

Zustimmen
I (quite) agree with you (on that point).
You're (quite) right there.

Englische Grammatik im Überblick

G1 **Substantiv: Besonderheiten der Pluralbildung**

half – **halves**	self – **selves**	Aber: chief – **chiefs**
knife – **knives**	thief – **thieves**	roof – **roofs**
life – **lives**	wife – **wives**	photograph – **photographs**
potato – **potatoes**	Aber: photo – **photos**	mouse – **mice**
tomato – **tomatoes**	radio – **radios**	tooth – **teeth**

G2 **Substantiv: Singular oder Plural? Abweichungen vom Deutschen**

Immer Plural:
The **cattle are** on the way to the slaughterhouse. *das Vieh ist*
The **contents** of the boxes **were** not insured. *der Inhalt war*

Als "Gruppenwörter" dann Plural, wenn nicht die "Gruppe" als Ganzes, sondern die Summe ihrer Mitglieder gemeint ist:
The **Post Office / Government say** they've got emergency plans. *die Post/Regierung sagt*
Head Office have promised us . . . *die Zentrale hat uns versprochen*
The **staff are** working almost round the clock. *das Personal arbeitet*
Spain have never won the World Cup. *Spanien hat*

Immer Singular:
The **United Nations / United States seems** to be unable to solve that problem.
die Vereinten Nationen / Vereinigten Staaten scheinen außerstande zu sein

In der Regel Singular:
Five dollars/pounds/gallons/years **is** not enough. *fünf Dollar/Pfund/. . . sind nicht genug*

Weitere Besonderheiten:
57,000 Americans lost their **lives** in the Vietnam War. *verloren das Leben*
He never weighed more than 9 **stone**.
Umgangssprachlich:
If anyone else does the same thing, I'll sack **them** (*statt des ebenfalls richtigen* him).

G3 **Das Adjektiv als Pluralsubstantiv**

Ex-Postal Worker Willed Millions to **(the) Blind**. *hinterließ Millionen den Blinden*
The dog that came back from **the dead**. *von den Toten*
Tax cuts for **the poor / the rich / the wealthy** *Steuersenkungen für die Armen/Reichen*

G4 **Angehörige von Nationen, Staaten usw. in Singular und Plural**

an Australian	two Australians	the Australians	Australians
an Austrian	two Austrians	the Austrians	Austrians
a Canadian	two Canadians	the Canadians	Canadians
a European	two Europeans	the Europeans	Europeans
a German	two Germans	the Germans	Germans
a New Zealander	two New Zealanders	the New Zealanders	New Zealanders
a Briton	two Britons	the British	British people

an Englishman/Englishwoman a Frenchman/Frenchwoman an Irishman/Irishwoman a Welshman/Welshwoman	two Englishmen/-women two Frenchmen/-women two Irishmen/-women two Welshmen/-women	the English the French the Irish the Welsh	English people French people Irish people Welsh people
a Scot(sman)/Scot(swoman)	two Scots(men/-women)	the Scots	Scottish people / Scots
a Chinese a Japanese a Swiss	two Chinese two Japanese two Swiss	the Chinese the Japanese the Swiss	Chinese people Japanese people Swiss people

G5 **One = "man"**

How can **one** prove **one's** loss to the insurance company? *wie kann man seinen Verlust beweisen*
Whether **one** is a vegetarian or not has no influence on **one's** character. *ob man Vegetarier ist*
One can't enjoy **oneself** if **one** is too tired. *man kann sich nicht amüsieren, wenn man*

G6 **Vom Deutschen abweichender Gebrauch der Possessivpronomen**

I don't like eating with **my** fingers. *mit den Fingern*
You should have **your** eyes tested. *solltest dir die Augen testen lassen*
The assistant just shrugged **his/her** shoulders. *zuckte nur mit den Achseln*
I fell down the stairs and almost broke **my** neck. *und brach mir fast den Hals / das Genick*
He's got **his** right leg in plaster. *er hat das rechte Bein in Gips*
He always has a loaded gun in **his** pocket. *in der Tasche*
She lost **her** temper. *verlor die Beherrschung*

Young people in **their** twenties *in den Zwanzigerjahren*
Even in **his** old age he drank 50 cups of coffee daily. *selbst im Alter*

G7 **Relativsätze**

Relativpronomen whose:
The woman **whose** daughter had bought the jeans was very polite. *die Frau, deren Tochter*

Relativpronomen whom (vorwiegend Schriftsprache):
Al Jolson was "The Singing Fool" **whom** many called the world's greatest entertainer.

Arten von Relativsätzen:
Bestimmender, einschränkender, d. h. für das Verständnis des Hauptsatzes notwendiger Relativsatz (keine Sprechpausen, keine Kommas):
The sweet old lady **who lives next door** was in an automobile accident while we were gone.
Nicht bestimmender, lediglich erläuternder, d. h. für das Verständnis des Hauptsatzes entbehrlicher Relativsatz (mit Sprechpausen und Kommas):
My husband's brother, **who is a doctor,** was in an automobile accident while we were gone.

G8 **Unterschiede zwischen some und any**

Grundregel: Some steht in bejahten Aussagen; any wird bei Verneinung und in Fragen gebraucht: He knows **something**. He doesn't know **anything**. Does he know **anything**?
Some steht auch in der Frageform und verneinten Form, wenn der Sinn der Aussage bejahend ist: Doesn't he know **something**? (I think he does!) Why doesn't she try to talk **some** sense into him? (I think she should!) Won't you have **some** coffee? (I'm sure you'd like some.)
Any steht auch in Nicht-Fragesätzen und nicht-verneinten Sätzen, wenn Ungewißheit über das Vorhandensein der bezeichneten Sache/Person zum Ausdruck gebracht werden soll: If **anyone** else does the same thing, I'll sack them.
Any steht auch zum Ausdruck von "niemand/nichts bestimmtes", "jede(r, s) x-beliebige": I can drink **anyone** under the table. The electronic display makes it possible for you to correct **any** mistakes before the text is actually printed out. *etwaige Fehler*

G9 **"Auch"**

Bejahtes "auch": There were jobs for vets' assistants and there were other jobs **too** / **as well**.
Verneintes "auch": There were no jobs for vets' assistants and there weren't any other jobs **either**.

G10 **Gebrauch der Zeiten für Gegenwart und Vergangenheit (Übersicht)**

Präsens einfach **Präsens Verlaufsform** ("gerade", "jetzt", "vorübergehend")	They **live** in London. They **are living** in London.	*sie wohnen in London* *sie wohnen (z. Z.) in London*
Präteritum einfach **Präteritum Verlaufsform** ("damals gerade/vorübergehend")	They **lived** in London. They **were living** in London.	*sie wohnten in London* *sie wohnten (damals gerade/noch) in London*
Perfekt (Handlung abgeschlossen) **Perfekt** (Handlung begann in der Vergangenheit und dauert noch an)	They **have moved** to London. They **have been living** in London for five years / since 1978.	*sie sind nach L. gezogen* *sie wohnen seit fünf Jahren / seit 1978 in London*
Plusquamperfekt (Handlung vor best. Zeitpunkt i. d. Vergangenheit bereits abgeschlossen) **Plusquamperfekt** (Handlung dauerte zu best. Zeitpkt. in der Vergangenheit noch an)	When I first met them, they **had** just **moved** to London. When I first met them, they **had been living** in London for six months.	*waren sie gerade nach London gezogen* *wohnten sie seit einem halben Jahr in London*
Weitere Beispiele zum Plusquamperfekt: He was told that his reservation **had been cancelled** by mistake. The police stopped the car because it **had been going** from side to side.		

G11 **Bedingungssätze: Die drei Grundtypen**

Typ 1	**If-Satz: Präsens**	**Hauptsatz: will + Infinitiv**
	If we **leave** at two, *Wenn wir um zwei abfahren,*	we **will** / we'**ll get** there at five. *werden wir um fünf dort ankommen.*
Typ 2	**If-Satz: Präteritum**	**Hauptsatz: would + Infinitiv**
	If we **left** at two, *Wenn wir um zwei abführen,*	we **would** / we'**d get** there at five. *würden wir um fünf dort ankommen.*
Typ 3	**If-Satz: had + Partizip Perfekt**	**Hauptsatz: would have + Partizip Perfekt**
	If we **had left** at two, *Wenn wir um zwei abgefahren wären,*	we **would have got** there at five. *wären wir um fünf dort angekommen.*

Gelegentlich findet sich im Nebensatz auch unless (≈ if . . . not):
You can't achieve real fluency in English **unless** you spend (≈ if you don't spend) some time in an English-speaking country.

G12 **Stellung des indirekten Objekts bei Verben mit zwei Objekten**

	Indirektes Objekt	Direktes Objekt	**Indirektes Objekt**
She gave/sold/promised/showed/offered	**Bill**	a ticket.	
She gave/sold/promised/showed/offered		a ticket	**to Bill**.

Faustregel: Das längere und/oder betontere Objekt steht meist hinten. Steht das indirekte Objekt hinter dem direkten Objekt, so geht ihm stets *to* voraus.

> He explained/demonstrated/described his method **to them.**

Explain, demonstrate und *describe* gehören zu einer kleinen Zahl von Verben, nach denen das indirekte Objekt nur mit *to* stehen kann. Also nicht: **He explained them his method.*

G13 **Typische Passivkonstruktionen (Übersicht)**

Präsens einfach **Präsens Verlaufsform**	The plans **are** often **changed**. The plans **are being changed**.	*werden oft geändert* *werden (gerade) geändert*
Präteritum einfach **Präteritum Verlaufsform**	The plans **were changed**. The plans **were being changed**.	*wurden geändert* *wurden (gerade) geändert*
Perfekt **Plusquamperfekt**	The plans **have been changed**. The plans **had been changed**.	*sind geändert worden* *waren geändert worden*
Will-Futur **Nach modalen Hilfsverben** **Nach have to**	The plans **will be changed**. The plans **can/must/should be changed**. The plans **had to be changed**.	*werden geändert werden* *können/müssen/sollten geändert werden* *mußten geändert werden*
To-Infinitiv **-ing-Form**	It's time for the plans **to be changed**. Is there any possibility of the plans **being changed**?	*es ist Zeit, daß die Pläne geändert werden* *besteht (irgend)eine Möglichkeit, daß die Pläne geändert werden?*

Frage nach dem Urheber: **Who** were the plans changed **by**? *von wem wurden die Pläne geändert?*
Persönliches Passiv (direktes Objekt als Subjekt der Passivkonstruktion): **They told** **me** that he had died about a week later. **I** **was told** that he had died about a week later. *man sagte mir*

G14 **Modale Hilfsverben und bedeutungsverwandte Ausdrücke**

Shall – should – ought to – be to – be supposed to **Shall** I/we tell them you can't come? *soll ich / sollen wir?* What **shall** I tell them? / What **am I to** tell them? *was soll ich ihnen sagen?* Let's go for a walk when this is over, **shall** we? *laß(t) uns . . . ja?* (Altmodisch-formell:) The right of the people to keep and bear arms **shall** not be infringed. (Gehoben-literarisch:) The future you **shall** know when it has come; before then, forget it. What clothes would you take along if you **were to / should** visit Alice Springs in January? Surely a bank like that **ought to / should** have an alarm system. *müßte/sollte (doch) eigentlich* What **is** the new drug **supposed to** do? *was soll das neue Medikament bewirken?* The curtains **were supposed to** have been dry-cleaned. *hatten gereinigt werden sollen*
Need not – (don't) have to – (don't) need to – must not Are your children as good at English as they **need/have to** be in this modern world? As long as you stay active, you **need not** worry / **don't have/need to** worry about losing your ability to learn. *brauchst du dir keine Sorgen zu machen* You **needn't** do that / **don't have/need to** do that. *brauchst das nicht zu tun* You **must not / mustn't** ['mʌsnt] do that. *darfst das nicht tun*

G15 **Modales Hilfsverb + Infinitiv des Perfekts**

I **could have kicked** myself. *"hätte mich treten können"* The robbers **may have got** away with tens of millions of pounds. *sind vielleicht entkommen* That **must have been** a hell of a job. *muß . . . gewesen sein* The money **should have been** spent on something else. *"hätte . . . ausgegeben werden sollen"* What **would** you **have done**? *was hättest du getan?* That **wouldn't have been** enough. *das wäre nicht genug gewesen*

G16 **Besonderheiten des Gebrauchs von do**

Keine do-Umschreibung, wenn ein Fragewort Subjekt oder Teil des Subjekts ist: Who **sold** my daughter this rubbish? What kind of people **come** here?
"Emphatisches" do zur Verstärkung der Aussage: If you've got a job for me, please '**do** let me know without delay. We '**do** hope that you'll be able to come to our country and visit us. Three months later she '**did** see the mongrel again.

G17 **Frage und Verneinung bei have**

Have wird in Frage und Verneinung normalerweise mit do umschrieben:
Where **did you have** lunch? *wo habt ihr zu Mittag gegessen?*
We **don't have** a car. *wir haben keinen Wagen*
It would be bad if we **didn't have** a car. *es wäre schlimm, wenn wir keinen Wagen hätten*

In Verbindung mit dem Partizip Perfekt wird selbstverständlich nie mit do umschrieben:
Have you written to Sandra? **Have you got** a car? We **haven't got** a car.

G18 **Hilfsverben als Hauptverb-Stellvertreter**

Hilfsverben können als "Pro-Formen" an die Stelle eines (bereits aufgetretenen) Hauptverbs oder längeren verbalen Ausdrucks treten:
Danny spends most of his spare time playing around with his computer. – 'All the kids **do** these days, don't they?
Has anyone got a camera? – (Yes,) 'I **have**.
Does anyone have a camera? – (Yes,) 'I **do**.
Would you like to work at night as 'he **does**? – No, I **'wouldn't**.
If anything can possibly go wrong today, it **'will**.
Fruit juices, wet fish and natural jams are the order of the day, and 'so **are** bran, wholemeal, and brown rice.
I love the dog. – So **do** 'I. / 'I **do** too.
I can't type. – Nor **can** 'I. / 'I **can't** either.

G19 **Der Infinitiv**

Nach Fragewörtern:
The question is who **to ask**. The problem is how **to be** in the right place at the right time.
In relativsatzähnlicher Funktion:
That'll give us something **to look** forward to.
Nach it:
It's wrong **to rear** animals only to kill them for food.
It takes no time **to get** someone to a trouble spot.
Nach bestimmten Verben, Substantiven und Adjektiven:
I can't afford **to lose** my driving licence. All their efforts **to open** the lock failed.
He was extremely lucky **to survive** the crash.
Nach Verb + Objekt und in der entsprechenden Passivkonstruktion:
They allowed the camels **to go** wild. The camels were allowed **to go** wild.
Nach for + Substantiv/Pronomen:
We've got plenty of room for Ann/her **to stay** with us.
Zum Ausdruck des Zwecks:
They went **to check** but found nothing wrong.
Im Passiv:
There was no one **to be seen** anywhere. It will have **to be sent in** for repair.
Infinitiv des Perfekts:
Tests of the drug are said **to have been** successful.
The curtains were supposed **to have been** dry-cleaned.

G20 **Die -ing-Form**

Als Subjekt:
Learning does not become more difficult with age.
Als Prädikativ:
Her only hobby is **painting**.
Nach bestimmten Verben:
I wouldn't mind/enjoy **spending** my Christmas holiday on some Australian beach.
Allgemein nach Präpositionen:
We look forward to **seeing** you in March. The locksmith succeeded in **opening** the door.
There are several ways of **doing** it. The bag is useful for **carrying** things bought on a trip.
He was charged with **failing** to obey the lights.
This is the garage where I usually take my car for **servicing**.
I never do anything important without **reading** my horoscope first.
On **entering** their flat, they got a nasty surprise.
You start the machine by **pressing** this button here.
In relativsatzähnlicher Funktion:
We have received hundreds of letters **supporting** our decision.
Everyone not **living** in the tropics is painfully aware that we are moving into another ice age.
There were birds **singing** in the trees.
Brenda, **sitting** alongside, looks into a mirror which has two pieces of tape stuck on it.
Als Adverbial:
He spends most of his spare time **playing** around with his computer.
The children fell asleep while **watching** TV.
His boss came in **demanding** to know about an order for 20 tins of floor polish.
With the children **playing** football there, we're getting balls kicked into our garden all the time.
Mit eigenem Sinnsubjekt:
When he's hungry, nothing will stop him **crying** until he gets his bottle.
If you want a picture of the future, imagine a boot **stamping** on a human face.
Some people are very much against companies such as McDonald's **opening** branches in their town.
Im Passiv:
Animals are often treated cruelly before **being slaughtered**.
There is some danger of a nuclear war **being started**.
Als echtes Substantiv:
If all people became vegetarians, that would not prevent the **killing** of animals.
There's so much **shouting** and **fighting** I'm afraid the neighbours will hear it.

G21 **Das Partizip Perfekt**

Nach Verb + Objekt:
I must have my hair **cut**. He got his motorcycle **repaired**.
A neighbour of ours had her wooden fence **pulled down** and washing **stolen** off the line.
We're getting balls **kicked** into our garden all the time.
Some Americans would like to see gun-handling courses **introduced** at high schools.
In relativsatzähnlicher Funktion:
A motorist **caught** drunk at the wheel may lose his licence.
The state of *1984* is a totalitarian police state **ruled** by an all-powerful "Big Brother".
Als Adverbial:
Asked to give a sample of his breath for analysis, Smith refused.
If **caught** in the early stages, this kind of cancer can be cured.
The remaining letters, when **put** in the right order, are an English proverb.
Given some knowledge of English to begin with, it is not too difficult a task to become fluent.

Namenverzeichnis

f = feminine Christian name
m = masculine Christian name
s = surname

Adelaide ['ædəleɪd]	the capital of South Australia, pop. 900,000
Africa ['æfrɪkə]	Afrika
Alice('s Adventures) in Wonderland	a story for children by Lewis Carroll, 1865
Alice Springs ['ælɪs 'sprɪŋz]	a town in central Australia, pop. 14,150
Arendt ['ɑːrənt]	Hannah (1906–75), German-American political theorist
Arnold ['ɑːnəld]	*m, s*
Atlanta [ət'læntə]	the capital of the U.S. state of Georgia, pop. 425,022
Atlantic (Ocean) [ət'læntɪk 'əʊʃn]	Atlantik; Atlantischer Ozean
Australia [ɒ'streɪljə]	Australien
Australian [ɒ'streɪljən]	australisch; Australier(in)
Ayers Rock ['eəz 'rɒk]	the world's largest monolith, in central Australia
Balzac ['bælzæk]	Honoré de (1799–1850), French novelist
Battersea ['bætəsɪ]	part of the south London borough of Wandsworth
the Beatles ['biːtlz]	British rock group of the nineteen sixties
Bentham ['bentəm]	Jeremy (1748–1832), English philosopher
Botany Bay ['bɒtənɪ 'beɪ]	("Botanik-Bucht") where Captain Cook first landed in Australia (1770), now surrounded by the airport and industrial Sydney
Byron ['baɪərən]	Lord George Gordon Noel (1788–1824), English romantic poet
Cambridge ['keɪmbrɪdʒ]	an English university town, 55 miles north of London
Canada ['kænədə]	Kanada
Canadian [kə'neɪdjən]	kanadisch; Kanadier(in)
the Canary Islands [kə'neərɪ]	die Kanarischen Inseln
Cape Town ['keɪp taʊn]	legislative and commercial centre of South Africa, pop. 1,096,000 (Kapstadt)
Croly ['krəʊlɪ]	David Goodman (1829–89), U.S. journalist
Darwin ['dɑːwɪn]	the capital of the Northern Territory, Australia, pop. 50,000
Decca ['dekə]	The Decca Record Co. Ltd., founded 1929
Dianne [daɪ'æn]	*f*
Dorothy ['dɒrəθɪ]	*f*
Edinburgh ['edɪnbrə]	the capital of Scotland, pop. 457,000
Edwards ['edwədz]	*s*
Einstein ['aɪnstaɪn]	Albert (1879–1955), German-born U.S. physicist
Europe ['jʊərəp]	Europa
Flynn [flɪn]	John (1880–1951), Australian clergyman
Geoff(rey) ['dʒef(rɪ)]	*m*
Georgia ['dʒɔːdʒjə]	a state in the SE U.S., pop. 5,464,265
Greek [griːk]	griechisch; Griechisch
Greenwich ['grɪnɪdʒ]	borough of SE Greater London, pop. 205,000
Hamlet ['hæmlɪt]	a tragedy by Shakespeare, 1601
Harrods ['hærədz]	a leading London department store, in Knightsbridge
Hatton Garden ['hætn 'gɑːdn]	a street in London EC1
Hilary ['hɪlərɪ]	*f*
Kennedy ['kenɪdɪ]	John Fitzgerald (1917–63), U.S. President (1961–63)
Kennesaw ['kenɪsɔː]	a town in the U.S. state of Georgia, pop. 5,095
King [kɪŋ]	Billie Jean (born 1943), U.S. tennis player
Lardner ['lɑːdnə]	Dionysius (1793–1859), professor of natural philosophy and astronomy, University College, London

Leonardo da Vinci [liːə'nɑːdəʊ dɑː 'vɪntʃiː]	(1452–1519) Italian artist, scientist, and engineer
Lincoln ['lɪŋkən]	Abraham (1809–65), U.S. President (1861–65)
Liverpool ['lɪvəpuːl]	a city in NW England, pop. 537,000
Marge [mɑːdʒ]	*f* (from Margery, Marjorie)
Marjorie ['mɑːdʒərɪ]	*f*
McLean [mə'kleɪn]	*s*
Melbourne ['melbən]	the capital of Victoria, SE Australia, pop. 2,480,000
Molière ['mɒlɪeə]	(1622–73) French dramatist
Mortimer ['mɔːtɪmə]	*s*
NATO ['neɪtəʊ]	North Atlantic Treaty Organization, established 1952
New Zealand [njuː 'ziːlənd]	Neuseeland
Northern Territory ['nɔːðn 'terɪtrɪ]	Territory of Australia, pop. 118,000
Orwell ['ɔːwəl]	George (1903–50), English writer
Patcham ['pætʃəm]	a village north of Brighton, East Sussex, England
Portsmouth ['pɔːtsməθ]	a port on the English south coast, pop. 190,000
Powell ['paʊəl]	*s*
Reagan ['reɪgən]	Ronald Wilson (born 1911), U.S. President (1981–)
Richmond ['rɪtʃmənd]	a suburb of Melbourne, Australia
Rio de Janeiro [riːəʊ də dʒə'nɪərəʊ]	the main port of Brazil, pop. 4,858,000
Robinson ['rɒbɪnsən]	*s*
the Rolling Stones ['rəʊlɪŋ 'stəʊnz]	British rock group formed in the early nineteen sixties
Russia ['rʌʃə]	Rußland
Scotland ['skɒtlənd]	Schottland
Shakespeare ['ʃeɪkspɪə]	William (1564–1616), English dramatist and poet
Shanklin ['ʃæŋklɪn]	a town in the Isle of Wight, pop. 7,480
Shaw [ʃɔː]	George Bernard (1856–1950), Irish-born British dramatist
The Singing Fool ['sɪŋɪŋ 'fuːl]	one of the first sound films, starring Al Jolson, U.S.A. 1928
South Australia ['saʊθ ɒ'streɪljə]	a State in S Australia, pop. 1,294,000
Spanish ['spænɪʃ]	spanisch; Spanisch
Susan ['suːzn]	*f*
Torquay [tɔː'kiː]	a town in SW England, part of Torbay, pop. 109,000
Tracey ['treɪsɪ]	*f*
Vienna [vɪ'enə]	Wien
Vietnam [vjet'næm]	Vietnam
Voltaire ['vɒlteə]	(1694–1778) French philosopher and writer
Wales [weɪlz]	part of Great Britain, pop. 2,775,000
Welsh [welʃ]	walisisch; Walisisch
the West Indies [west 'ɪndɪz]	die Westindischen Inseln; Westindien
the Isle of Wight ['aɪl əv 'waɪt]	an island off the English south coast, pop. 117,000
Zurich ['zjʊərɪk]	Zürich

Grammatikregister mit Begriffserklärungen

Adjektiv (Eigenschaftswort, adjective) G3
Adverb (Umstandswort) 8C1, 12C1
any – some 11C1, G8
"auch" 3A, 12C2, G9
auxiliaries (Hilfsverben, Hilfszeitwörter) 4C1, 5C1, G14, G15, G18
be supposed to G14
be to G14
Bedingungssatz 1C, 2D1, 4B2, 4C3, 5C2, 10C2, 12B4, 15C1, G11
Beifügungssatz (Relativsatz, relative clause) 4C2, 6C, 11C2, G7
besitzanzeigende Fürwörter (Possessivpronomen, possessive adjectives) G6
Bezugs(wort)satz (Relativsatz, relative clause) 4C2, 6C, 11C2, G7
catenatives 8C2, G19, G20
concord (Kongruenz, Übereinstimmung zwischen Subjekt und Prädikat) 7C1, G2
conditional clause (Konditionalsatz, Bedingungssatz) 1C, 2D1, 4B2, 4C3, 5C2, 10C2, 12B4, 15C1, G11
do(n't) G16
Einzahl – Mehrzahl 7C1, G1
either – too 3A, G9
Ergänzung (Objekt, object) G12
Frageanhängsel (question tags) 15C2
Gerundium (Verbalsubstantiv, substantivisch gebrauchte *-ing*-Form) 3C1, 3C2, 8C2, 9C2, G20
get/have + Subst. + Part. Perf. 9A, 9C1, G21
Grundform 8C2, 9C2, G15, G19
have 9A, 9C1, G17, G21
have/get + Subst. + Part. Perf. 9A, 9C1, G21
have to G14
Hilfsverben (Hilfszeitwörter, auxiliaries) 5C1, G14, G15, G18
if clause (*if*-Satz) 1C, 2D1, 4B2, 4C3, 5C2, 10C2, 12B4, 15C1, G11
indirect speech (indirekte/nichtwörtliche/berichtete Rede, reported speech) 10C1
indirekte Rede (nichtwörtliche/berichtete Rede, indirect/reported speech) 10C1
indirektes Objekt (Dativobjekt, indirect object) G12
Infinitiv (Grundform, Nennform, infinitive) 8C2, 9C2, G15, G19
Infinitiv d. Perfekts (perfect infinitive) 4C1, 4C3, 5C1, 5C2, 10C2, 12B4, 15C1, G11, G15, G19
-ing-Form 3C1, 3C2, 6C, 8C2, 9C2, G20
irregular verbs Umschlagseite 3
Konditional(satz) (Bedingungssatz, conditional clause) 1C, 2D1, 4B2, 4C3, 5C2, 10C2, 12B4, 15C1, G11
Kongruenz (Übereinstimmung zwischen Subjekt u. Prädikat, agreement) 7C1, G2
"lassen" 9A, 9C1, G21
Leideform (Passiv, passive) G13, G19, G20
-ly-Adverbien 8C1, 12C1
"man" G5
Mehrzahl – Einzahl 7C1, G1
Mittelwort d. Gegenwart (Partizip Präsens, Präsenspartizip, *-ing*-Form, present participle) 6C, 9C2, G20
Mittelwort d. Vergangenheit (Partizip Perfekt, Perfektpartizip, past participle) 4C1, 5C1, 5C2, 6C, 9A, 9C1, 12B4, 15C1, G21
modal auxiliaries (modale Hilfsverben/Hilfszeitwörter, Modalverben) 4C1, 5C1, G14, G15, G18
modale Hilfsverben (Hilfszeitwörter, Modalverben, modal auxiliaries) 4C1, 5C1, G14, G15, G18
must not G14
Nationalitätsbezeichnungen G4
need G14
Nennform (Grundform, Infinitiv, infinitive) 8C2, 9C2, G15, G19
nor – so 3A, 12C2
noun = Substantiv, Hauptwort
number (Numerus, grammatische Zahl) 7C1, G2
Numerus (grammatische Zahl, number) 7C1, G2
Objekt ([Satz-]Ergänzung, object) G12
one = "man" G5
ought to G14
Partizip Perfekt (Perfektpartizip, Mittelwort d. Vergang., past participle) 4C1, 5C1, 5C2, 6C, 9A, 9C1, 12B4, 15C1, G21
Partizip Präsens (Präsenspartizip, Mittelwort d. Gegenw., *-ing*-Form, present participle) 6C, 9C2, G20
Passiv (Leideform, passive) G13, G19, G20
passive voice (Passiv, Leideform) G13, G19, G20
past participle (Partizip Perfekt, Perfektpartizip, Mittelwort d. Vergang.) 4C1, 5C1, 5C2, 6C, 9A, 9C1, 12B4, 15C1, G21
past perfect (Plusquamperfekt, vollendete Vergangenheit) G10, G13
perfect infinitive (Infinitiv d. Perfekts) 4C1, 4C3, 5C1, 5C2, 10C2, 12B4, 15C1, G11, G15, G19
Perfekt (vollendete Gegenwart, present perfect tense) 2C, 7C2, 7C3, 14C, G10, G13

Perfektpartizip (Partizip Perfekt, Mittelwort d. Vergang., past participle) 4C1, 5C1, 5C2, 6C, 9A, 9C1, 12B4, 15C1, G21
Plural (Mehrzahl) – Singular (Einzahl) 7C1, G1
Plusquamperfekt (vollendete Vergangenheit, past perfect) G10, G13
possessive adjectives (Possessivpronomen, besitzanz. Fürwörter) G6
Possessivpronomen (besitzanz. Fürwörter, possessive adjectives) G6
Präposition (Verhältniswort, preposition) 3C1, 3C2, 8C2, 9C2, G20
Präsenspartizip (Partizip Präsens, Mittelwort d. Gegenw., *-ing*-Form, present participle) 6C, 9C2, G20
Präteritum = Imperfekt, Vergangenheit(sform), past tense
preposition (Präposition, Verhältniswort) 3C1, 3C2, 8C2, 9C2, G20
present participle (Partizip Präsens, Präsenspartizip, Mittelwort d. Gegenw., *-ing*-Form) 6C, 9C2, G20
present perfect (Perfekt, vollendete Gegenwart) 2C, 7C2, 7C3, 14C, G10, G13
present tense = Präsens, Gegenwart(sform)
Pronomen = Fürwort, pronoun
pronoun = Pronomen, Fürwort
question tags (Frageanhängsel) 15C2
reflexive pronouns (*-self*-Pronomen, Reflexivpronomen, rückbezügl. Fürwörter) 13C
Reflexivpronomen (*-self*-Pronomen, rückbezügl. Fürwörter, reflexive pronouns) 13C
relative clause (Relativsatz, Bezugs[wort]satz, Beifügungssatz) 4C2, 6C, 11C2, G7
relative pronoun = Relativpronomen, bezügliches Fürwort
Relativpronomen = bezügliches Fürwort, relative pronoun
Relativsatz (Bezugs[wort]satz, Beifügungssatz, relative clause) 4C2, 6C, 11C2, G7
reported speech (indirekte/nichtwörtliche/berichtete Rede, indirect speech) 10C1
rückbezügliche Fürwörter (*-self*-Pronomen, Reflexivpronomen, reflexive pronouns) 13C
Satzergänzung (Objekt, object) G12
-self-Pronomen (Reflexivpronomen, rückbezügl. Fürwörter, reflexive pronouns) 13C
shall G14
should(n't) 4C1, G14
Singular (Einzahl) – Plural (Mehrzahl) 7C1, G1
so – nor 3A, 12C2
some – any 11C1, G8
Substantiv = Hauptwort, noun
tag questions (Frageanhängsel) 15C2
Tempora ([grammat.] Zeiten, tenses) 14C, G10, G13
tenses (Tempora, [grammat.] Zeiten) 14C, G10, G13
to-Infinitiv 8C2, 9C2, G19
to-Objekt G12
too – either 3A, G9
Umstandswort (Adverb) 8C1, 12C1
unless G11
unregelmäßige Verben Umschlagseite 3
verb = Verb, Zeitwort, "Tätigkeitswort"
Verhältniswort (Präposition, preposition) 3C1, 3C2, 8C2, 9C2, G20
Völkernamen G4
vollendete Gegenwart (Perfekt, present perfect) 2C, 7C2, 7C3, 14C, G10, G13
vollendete Vergangenheit (Plusquamperfekt, past perfect) G10, G13
whom G7
whose G7
would 1C, 2D1, 4B2, 4C2, 5C2, 10C2, 12B4, 15C1, G11
Zeiten (Tempora, tenses) 14C, G10, G13

Wortschatzregister

Bei den schräggedruckten Einträgen handelt es sich um Wörter aus *Welcome 1–2*, die im vorliegenden Band mit leicht veränderter Bedeutung bzw. in anderen typischen Fügungen oder abweichenden Formen vorkommen.

ability 7B
Aboriginal 6B
above 3B
accept 1B
acceptable 9B
accidental(ly) 13B
accompany 6B
account 5B, 15B
act 3B
action 15B
active 8B
actor 3B
actress 3B
actual 9B
ad 1C
addressed 1B
adult 1D
adult-education centre 13D
advanced 8B
advert 1D
advice 4B
advise 9C
aeroplane 10B
afterwards 1A
aged 8B
agency 3B
agent 11B
aggressive 4B
ago 9B
agreement 7B
ahead 10B
aid 13D
airmail 11A
airplane 7A
alarm system 5B
alcohol 2B
alcoholic 2D
alibi 11D
alike 11A
alive 3D
all 7B
along 6A
alongside 3B
alter 9A
amateur 5C
amen 13B
amendment 13B
among 5B
analysis 2B
ancient 6B
another 2B
apologize 15D
apology 15C
apparently 5B
appeal 3B
appear 5B
appetizing 12B
apply 12C, 15B
appreciate 14B
apprenticeship 14A
architect 15B

area 1B, 9B
argue 9D
argument 8B
armed services 13B
arms 13B
arrangement 1D
arrest 7A
article 7B
artificial 7A
ashamed 2B
assistant 3B
association 13B
at long last 5B
atomic 7B
attack 4B, 7B
attendant 4A
attention 4B
audio 8B
author 10B
automobile 14B
Ave. (= Avenue) 1B
average 12D
avoid 10A
award 15C
aware 10B

baby-sitting 1B
back 1B
bag 2A
baggage 11A
bake 12A
balance 7B
ball 3B, 10B
ball pen 11A
ban 7B, 13B
bare 6A
base 6A
battery 11B
battery production 12B
be to 6A
bear 13B
beat 10B
before 15B
begin 8B
beside 5B
besides 9B
beware 13B
beyond 4B, 12D
Bible 10B
birch 13D
blackmail 10B
blasted 1B
bless 14B
blind 7A
blood 2A
blow 2A
boast 2D
bodyguard 13B
book 15C
boom 12B
boot 10B

border 11A
bother 2B
bottom 6B
bounce 3B
boxing match 11A
brackets 5A
brain 8B
bran 12B
break 1B, 9B, 11B, 14D
breakdown 4B
breath 2A
breathe 10C
breed 13D
brewery 9D
bring about 7B
brisk 13B
British Rail 9D
brochure 1D
brown 12B
bruise 11B
brush up 8D
bugger off 15B
builder 2B
built-in 11B
bungalow 9B
bunker 7B
burglar 1D
burglary 13B
burn 7B
bury 6C
bush 6B, 9B
business 4B
button 7B
by 4D

cage 12D
calculator 11A
calf 7A
calories 12A
camel 6B
camping area 1B
cancel 4B
cancer 10B
caravan 1A
care 4B
career 3B
careful(ly) 13C
careless 5C
carpet 15B
cartoon movie 14B
catalogue 7B
catch 2A
cause 4B
celebrate 2B
cellar 7B
cent 11A
century 10B
champion 10B
channel 7A
chap 6B
charge 2B, 7A, 15B

charter 6B
chat 1B
cheers 2B
chemical 12D
chew 12A
choice 3B
choose 1A
circle 13A
circular 8B
circumstances 15C
citizen 8B
City 5B
city hall 13B
classroom 1A
claw 3B
clean out 5B
clear 2B, 7B
clever 5B
climb 6A
clipping 14B
close 11C
closed-circuit TV 5B
closely 4A
cloth 5A
cloud 7B
coal 7B
Coke 4D
college 8A
coloured 3B
combine 13B
comment 10B, 11D
common 10B
commonly 13B
community 13B
compensation 15C
compile 13B
complain 4B
complaint 4A, 15B
composition 7A
computer 4B
condition(al) 4C
conference 5D
confusing 15A
congratulate 6B
congress 11A
consider 1A, 3D
constable 2B
constitution 13B
consume 12B
consumer 4B
contain 5D
content 3C
contents 5C
continue 7B
control 4B, 10B
convenience food 12B
convict 15B
convince 8D
cottage 1B
cotton 5A
council 9B
countless 10B

courage 15B
court 1D, 2B
cover 5A, 6B
cow 11A
crash 2B
crazy 11C
crime rate 13B
criminal 7B, 13B
cross off 5A
cruel 12D
crystal ball 10B
culture 6B
cup 4C
cure 10B
curtain 4A
cutlet 12B

damage 7B
dare 9B
darn 1B
dash 11B
daylight saving time 6A
deal 5A
deal with 4B
dealer 5B
decide 15B
decision 5B
declare 13B
decline 8B
decorate 14B
defeat 7C
defence 13D
defend 13B
defendant 2B
degree 1B
delay 3B
delightful 6B
demand 4A, 12B
democracy 10A
demonstrate 3B
depend 9B
deposit 1D
deserve 9B
design 3B
dessert 12B
destroy 7B, 12D
detective 15D
deterrence 7B
develop 2B
development 1B
device 10B
devil 12D
diagnose 6C
diamond 5B
dilemma 7B
discover 4A
discovery 10B
disease 6B
dismiss 15B
dismissal 15B
display 11B

Wortschatzregister

disqualify 2A
distance 6A
distant 6C
district 7B
disturb 6B
divorced 2B
dogs' home 1B
dole 3B
door 5B
downright 7B
downstairs 11B
draw 5A
drawer 14D
dress designer 4C
drink 2A
drink-driver 2D
drink-driving 2D
drive 10B, 13B
driver's test 14B
drop 2B
drug 2A
drunk 2A
dry-cleaner 4A
duck 12B
due 12B
dump 9B
dust 4D

ear 10B
earnings 2B
east 4B
eastern 2B
education 8D
effort 3B, 6B
e.g. 11B
either 2B
elderly 8B
electricity 10B
elementary 8B
employee 4B
empty 1D
enable 10B
enclose 8B
end 3B
end up 15B
enemy 7B
energy 7B
engineer 5B
enjoyment 12B
enter 6A, 14D
entrance test 8B
envelope 1B
equipment 8B, 9B
equipped 1B
establish 10B
estate 9D
estimate 13B
event 8D
ex- 7A
examine 7A
exchange 1D, 4A
exit 7B
exorbitant 4D
expand 3C
experienced 8B

explanation 4B
explosion 7B
extra 3B
extraordinary 12B

fail 5B, 15B
fair 1B
fair enough 9B
fairyland 14B
false 5B
fan 12A
fat 7B
fault 4B
favour 8B
fear 9B
feature 8B
fed up 15B
feelings 14B
fence 9A
fibre 12B
fight 2B, 7B
fill 9A
findings 1A
fine 2A, 2B
finished 2B
firearms 13B
flat 5A
floor 3B
floor polish 15B
flour 12B
fluency 8B
fluently 8B
folk 9B
folks 13C
fondly 14B
fool 7B
for 9B, 12B
forbid 2D
force 5B, 12D
forecast 1B, 10B
foreigner 8B
forever 14B
forgive 14B
fortunately 11A
forward 2B
founder 6C
free 1B
free-range eggs 12B
freeway 2A
freeze 1C
friendship 14B
front 15B
frugal 12B
function 8B
future 10B
futurologist 10B
futurology 10B

gallon 11A
gang 5D
gas 10B
general 8D
generous 9B
get out 2B
get out of 2B, 5B

give way 12B
given 8B
glimpse 10B
glory 6B
go on 14A
gold 1B
gone 14B
good-looking 3B
gradually 15B
grammar 8A
grand 11A, 15C
grandmaster 11C
greenhouse 9B
grounds 1B
growing pains 14B
guard 9D
guilty 2B
guitar 10C
gun 5B
gunshot wound 13B

habit 12A
hand over 13C
handgun 13B
handle 13B
hang around 9D
happening 14B
harbour 1B
hardly ever 4B
hate 9B
head office 4B
head-on 2B
health food 12A, 12B
healthy 10A
hear 2B
hearing 15C
heavy 12D
heavy going 3B
hell 5B
hen 12D
hesitate 15B
high school 13B
history 7B
hit 9B, 14B
hold 4B, 10C
hold up 2B
hole 9A
holocaust 7B
homestead 6B
honestly 3B
horizontal(ly) 3B
householder 13D
however 3B, 8B
human being 10B
humour 7B
hurry 6B

ice age 10B
ideal 1B
ill health 6B
illegal 13B
imagine 1B
immediately 4B
impress 11B
improve 7C, 8A

incidentally 11B
include 1D
inconvenience 4D
increase 2B
indeed 8B, 10B
independent 7C
industrial tribunal 15B
influence 2B
infringe 13B
inhumane(ly) 12D
insist 4A
inspect 3B
insufficient 9B
insure 5B
intelligence 13D
intend 8D
intensive 8A
interest 4B
interest rate 7C
intermediate 8D
interpret 8A
interrupt 4B
interview 5D
investment 1B
invitation 4B
invite 6C
involve 13B
IQ 11D

jacket 5A
jail 2A
jam 5B
jewel 5B
Jobcentre 3B
journal 10B
judge 10B, 15B
judgment 13C
jukebox 9D
jumble 13A
junction 15B
just like that 1B

keen 9B
keep 5C
keep up 12B
key 5B
kick 9B
kilogram 11B
kind 6B
knock 9B
know-how 8B
knowledge 8B

lager 2B
lamb 12B
land 5A, 10B
latest 8B
law 13B
law-abiding 13B
lawyer 2B
lay 12D
lay off 14B
lazy 14B
lead 7B, 7C
left 7B

length 4A
let out 9A
letter box 7B
level 8B
licence 2A
licensed 1B
light 9B
likely 10B
limit 2B
limited 3B
line 3B, 9B
litre 11A
load 13B
lobby 4B
lock 5B
locksmith 5B
lonely 3B
Lord 2B, 12B
lorry 4B
loss 5B
lot 7B
loud 4B
lounge 1B
lousy 4D
lower 2D
Ltd 4D

mad 1B
magistrates' court 2B
mail-order catalogue 7B
mail run 6B
major 7C
make 11D
make sure 2B
make up 7A
man-made 7A
manage 7B, 13D
manager 4B, 15B
manufacture 2D
marriage 2B
match 11A
material 3B
matter 4C
matter of course 13B
maximum 6A
mayor 13B
meaningful 6C
meet 14D
memory 11B
mend 9A
mention 3D
mess 14D
meter 15A
method 4B
Middle East 4B
mind 5A, 8B, 13B
mini- 10B
miracle 11B
mirror 3B
miss 11B
missing 5B
mistake 4B
mongrel 15B
mood 1D, 14B

moped 10B
motel 6B
motion picture 10B
motorcycle 9A
motorist 2A
mouldy 4A
mouse 3B
muffin 12B
murder 6B, 11A
mushroom cloud 7B
musical 8B
must not 3B

named 10B
nasty 2B
nation 7B
National Rifle Association 13B
nature 5A
neck 11B
need 8B
newly 4B
news item 2B
news story 5D
next to 2C
nights 3B
no one 5B
Nobel Prize 10B
non- 12D
nonsense 7B
nor 1B
normally 8B
note down 1A
notebook 7A
notice 5B
novel 10B
nowhere 9B
nuclear 7B
nuclear power plant 7B

obey 15B
obviously 5B
occasion 9B
off 9B, 10A
official 5B
only 13B
opponent 4B
order 12B, 13B
ordinary 10B
organization 4B
original 10B
otherwise 3A
ought 5B
oughtn't 5B
out of work 7C
outback 6B
outlaw 13B
outline 5D
outright 2B
over 2B, 11D
overseas 8B
own 3D, 10B
oyster 12A

packet 11B
painful 10B
paint 9A
pair 4B
particular 1B
particularly 5B
particulars 1B
partridge 12B
party 2B
pass 3B, 13B, 13C, 14B
past 10B
patrol 9B
pay off 3B
peace 7B
peaceful 1B
penalty 13D
personality 13A
philosopher 12B
photograph 6B
pick 1A
pick up 3B, 9B
picture 12D
pilot 6B
pipe 11A
pity 6B
place 8B
plains 6A
plant 9B
plaster 11B
plastic 4D
playground 9B
pleased 7A
plenty 5B
poem 8C
poet 10B
point 3B, 5B, 7D
point out 4B
poison 12B
police 2A
polish 9A, 15B
politician 7B
politics 11D
poll 1A
pollster 1A
pollution 7C
pony trekking 1A
pool 9D, 10B
pop music 5A
pork 12B
portable 10B
portion 12B
posh 1B
possession 13B
Post Office 7B
postal worker 7A
power 7B
powerful 10A
predecessor 13B
predict 10B
prediction 10B
preferably 3B
prepare 3B, 14B
prepared 3B
present 10B

press conference 5D
pressure 14B
prevent 2B
previous 15B
principal 8B
print 6A, 6B, 11B
printing shop 3B
prisoner 7A
proceeds 1B
produce 7B
producer 5A
professional 5B, 5C
professor 8B
profit 7A
progress 8B
project 6D
properly 11A
property 1B
pros and cons 1D
prosecution 2B
protect 1D
protection 4B
protest 9B
prove 5B
proverb 5A
provided 8B
psychologist 4B
publish 10B
pull 3B
pull down 9B
pull up 9B
punish 13B
pupil 8B
puppy 15B
pure 12B
purpose 6B
push 7B
put 14B
put down 15B
put on 3B, 4B
put up 1A
pyjamas 4B

queue 3B
quite 7B

radiation 7B
raid 5B
rail 4B
rainstorm 14B
rape 13B
raspberry 1A
rate 2D, 7C, 12D, 13B
rather 1B, 14B
react 7D
reaction 7A
read out 6D
realize 3B
rear 12D
reasonable 1B
reasonably 3B
receive 8B
recently 5B
recognize 15B
record 7A

recovery 11D
redecorate 9A
reduced 1B
reduction 1D
refuse 2B
regain 7C
regard 12D
regards 6B
regional 7B
regret 2B
relation 7C
relationship 1B
relative 14A
relatively 2B
relevant 13A
religion 6B
religious 10A
remark 12B
remnants 3B
renew 9A
repair 4A
repeat 10B
replace 4A
replacement 4A
reply 12B
reporter 5B
republic 11A
require 1D, 13B
requirements 1D
resident 9D
responsible 4B
restless 12D
result 4B
return 14B
rice 12B
ride 1D
rifle 13B
right 9B, 13B
risk 2B
rob 5B
robber 5B
robbery 5C, 13B
rock 6A
roof 9B
rose 11A
roughly 6B
routine 3B
row 7A
rubbish 4B
rubble 4D
ruin 4A
rule 10B
run 7B
run out of 3B

sack 15B
sad 14B
s.a.e. 1B
safe-deposit box 5B
safety 9B
sail 1C
salary 5A
sale 1B
salesman 2B
sample 2A

sand 5A
sandy 6B
satisfy 4A
sauce 12D
save 15B
science 5A
scientific 10B
scientist 7B
Scotch 2D
seam 4B
season 6A
secondary school 8A
secret 6D
seldom 6C
self-employed 2B
send in 4A
sender 1B
sense 2B
sentence 2A
separate 1A
set 10B
settler 6B
several 9B
sew 3A
sewing machine 3B
shall 13B
shape 14B
share 1B, 1D
shaver 4A
shelter 7B
ship 1A
shocked 7A
shoot 13B
should 8C
shout 2B, 4B
shower 1D
shrug 4A
shut out 5A
sign 13B
signpost 15A
silent 11B
silly 12D
since 9A
sincerely 14B
single 3B
site 1B
sitting room 9A
skill 3B
skilled 3B
skin 7A
sleep 4D
slim 12A
slip 11B
slogan 11D
smallpox 6B
smash 9B
smooth 5B
snow 14B
snow in 14C
sober 2A
sober up 2B
society 10B
soda water 12B
sofa 4B
solid 1B

solution 13B
solve 7B
somehow 4A
song 3B
sorry 4A
sort out 4B
sound 10C
source 10B
spare 1B
spare time 10A
specialist 4B
speedy 11D
spite 10B
split 4B
spokesman 9B
spot 7A, 9B
spread 1B
square 5A
square brackets 11B
stage 10B
stamp 10B
stamped 1B
stand 4B, 15A
station 6B
statistics 10B
steal 5B
step 11B
stick 3B
stockpile 7B
stone 12B
stop 15A
straight away 4B
strange 4A
strap 4B
stress 14B
striking 10B
string 3B
strongly 13B
strongroom 5B
structure 5C
struggle 7B
stuck 6B
stuff 2B, 12D
succeed 5D
success 2A
successful 2A
suffer 2A
suffering 15B
sugar 12B
suggestion 9B
summit 6A
sunglasses 1B
sun-powered plane 7A
sunrise 6A
sunset 6A
superpower 7B
supervisor 13B
supper 12A
supply 7B, 9D
support 8B
sure 2B
surely 5B
surgery 15B
surgery hours 15A
survive 6B
suspect 2A, 7A
sway 2A
swear 9B, 15B
switch 12B
sympathy 4B

take place 1B
talent 3B
tape 3B
taste 12B
taxpayer 10B
teach 3B
technical 8B
temper 15B
tent 1A
terrorist 10B
terrorize 9D
test 2A, 8B, 14B
that 7B
thaw 10B
theft 5B
thick 7B
thief 5B
think up 7B
third 11B
threaten 4B
throw 4D
tidy 3B
tie 3B
tied down 1D
tile 9B
time share 1B
tin 4D
tiny 11B
title 10B
tobacco 11A
ton 15B
tooth 9C
topic 13A
totalitarian 10B
tour operator 4D
towards 12B
toy 11B
trade 5B
Trades Union Congress 11A
tragic 2B
train 3B
transfer 5B
translation 3B
transport manager 15B
travel 6B
travel agent 11C
travel firm 4D
trend 10B
tribunal 15B
tropics 10B
trouble spot 9B
troubles 10B
true 10B
truly 3B
trust 7B
truth 10B
tuberculosis 6B
turn 15B
turn down 10C
turn out 14D

ulcer 14B
unable 10B
unconscious 9B
underline 4C
undress 4B
unemployed 7C
unless 1D
unload 15B
unlock 5B
unoccupied 1D
unspoiled 1B
unsprayed 12A
up 3B
up to 1D
us 12D
use 8D, 10B
used 3B
useless 5A

vaccinate 9A
valuable 5B
valuables 5B
vegetarian 12A
vegetarianism 12D
vehicle 10B
versus 13B
very 8B
vet's assistant 3B
visual 8B
vote 13D

wait 15A
wake up 3B
Walkman 11D
wallet 13C
warehouseman 15B
warning 15A
washing 9B
wasteland 9B
watch 4B
way 3B
wealthy 10B
weapon 7B
weekday 15A
weight 11D
welcome 8B
well-known 8B
well-mannered 14B
were 14B
wet fish 12B
wheel 2A
wholemeal 12B
whom 11A
whose 4C
widespread 10B
wild 6B
will 7A
willing 3B
wisdom 12D
wise 1B
wishes 14B
witness 2B
wonder 4A, 11B
wooden 9B
working order 13B
World Cup 4C
worthy 10B
wound 13B
wristwatch 11B

yet 12B
youngster 9B
yours truly 3B
youths 9B

zone 6A